SEAFOOD

FOR ALL SEASONS

BayBooks

An imprint of HarperCollins*Publishers*

A BAY BOOKS PUBLICATION
An imprint of HarperCollinsPublishers

First published in 1992 in Australia by Bay Books, of
CollinsAngus&Robertson Publishers Pty Limited (ACN 009 913 517)
A division of HarperCollinsPublishers (Australia) Pty Limited
25 Ryde Road, Pymble NSW 2073, Australia

HarperCollinsPublishers (New Zealand) Limited
31 View Road, Glenfield, Auckland 10, New Zealand

HarperCollinsPublishers Limited
77-85 Fulham Palace Road, London W6 8JB, United Kingdom

National Library of Australia
Cataloguing-in-Publication data:

   Seafood for all seasons.
   Includes index

   ISBN 1 86378 044 0

   1. Cookery (Seafood).
   (Series: Bay Books cookery collection)

   641.692

Front cover photograph by Quentin Bacon with styling by Donna Hay
(seafood supplied by Peter's Fish Market, Blackwattle Bay; plate supplied
by Orrefors Kosta Boda, Miranda)
Back cover and chapter opening photography by Quentin Bacon
with styling by Jennene Plummer
Back cover picture: Paella, recipe on page 52
(glasses by Primex Products Pty Ltd, Sydney)
Printed by Griffin Press Pty Ltd, Netley, South Australia

5 4 3 2 1
96 95 94 93 92

Contents

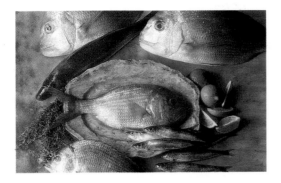

SEAFOOD FOR ALL SEASONS

How lucky we are to have such an abundance of seafood — to be able to go to a fishmonger, and choose from so many different varieties of fish, molluscs and crustaceans. All over the world, consumers can pick from any of the hundreds of species which arrive daily from various coastlines.

Seafood is available in many varieties and forms — from whole fish and fish cutlets to tiny shells and giant crabs. There are endless varieties, from blackfish to scorpionfish, and tuna to whiting, and freshwater fish to farmed fish. Seafood is seasonal, which means price varies according to season. Choose seafood which is in season for the best buys. Seafood not in season is often available, although it costs a lot more. Refer to the seafood reference chart for information.

SEAFOOD AND NUTRITION

Today, more and more people are becoming aware of the health benefits of eating fish.

- Not only is fish high in protein, minerals and vitamins, but research has shown that seafoods average less than 2% fat, which is much lower than most chicken cuts and lean red meat.
- The fat found in seafood is mostly polyunsaturated. In particular the polyunsaturated fatty acids in seafood are mainly omega 3 and some omega 6 which can lower the levels of some types of fat in the blood, reduce blood pressure and prevent clots from forming. This means reduced risk of heart attack and stroke. Omega 3 fatty acids have also helped to reduce inflammation in some skin conditions and in some types of arthritis. Omega 3 fatty acids are found in both fish and shellfish.
- All seafoods are low in kilojoules, and of course you do not have to trim any fat. Just grill, barbecue, bake, steam,

poach or microwave seafood to keep their low kilojoule count.

- All fish is low in cholesterol. Even prawns, often given the thumbs down, have almost no saturated fat. Eating fish 2 to 3 times a week can help lower excess cholesterol levels and reduce the risk of heart disease. It's no wonder doctors and nutritionists are encouraging us to eat more fish.

SHOPPING FOR FISH

The guide below is an indication of how much fish to buy per person per serve. Remember, this is only a guide — the type of eaters you are cooking for will determine the exact quantity you need to buy.

Per person:

- whole fish: 300–350 g
- whole fish (head removed and cleaned): 225–300 g
- fish fillets: 150–200 g
- fish cutlets: 200–250 g

GUIDELINES FOR PURCHASING FRESH SEAFOOD

Whole fish:

- look for bright bulging eyes, not sunken
- gills should be bright red
- flesh should be firm and elastic
- fish should have a pleasant sea smell
- skin should be lustrous and bright

Fish fillets and cutlets:

- should be shiny and firm, not dull and soft

- should have no discolouration
- water should not 'ooze' when touched
- should have a pleasant sea smell

Shellfish (crustaceans and molluscs): Shellfish can be purchased fresh or frozen. Fresh shellfish can be purchased cooked, raw or alive. To buy cooked or raw look for:

- shell intact
- no discolouration at joints
- pleasant sea smell

To buy alive look for:

- limbs intact
- active crustacean
- if buying live molluscs, shells should be closed

STORING FISH

Refrigerating fish:

- if fish is whole, scale and gut
- rinse fish in cold water; pat dry
- wrap in plastic wrap or foil, or place in a covered container
- store in refrigerator, use within 2 to 3 days

Refrigerating shellfish:

- place in a covered container
- store in refrigerator, use within 2 to 3 days
- live mussels, pipis, clams, cockles and oysters will die if placed in the refrigerator. Keep these in a damp hessian sack in a cool, dark place. Use within 3 days. Discard any that open prior to cooking and which do not close again after being tapped gently.

Freezing fish:

- make sure fish is as fresh as possible

- whole fish must be gutted; scales may be left on for freezing, as these will act as an insulator and help retain moisture
- wrap whole fish, fillets and cutlets in plastic wrap, then place into freezer bags
- remove air from the bag, seal and label
- fish can be frozen for 4 to 6 months

Freezing shellfish:

- prawns: place prawns (cooked or green) in a plastic container, cover with cold water, seal and freeze — forming an ice block; shells may be left intact, as they will act as an insulator.
- octopus, squid, cuttlefish: gut, clean and rinse well; place in freezer bag, exclude air, seal, label and freeze.
- crustaceans: keep shells intact., wrap in plastic wrap; place into a freezer bag, exclude air, seal and freeze.

PREPARATION OF FISH

Fish needs little preparation prior to cooking. Fish fillets and cutlets only need to be rinsed with cold water and patted dry. Whole fish though, needs a little more preparation, which your fishmonger can do for you free of charge.

To scale fish: fully immerse whole fish in cold water. Hold fish firmly by the tail and with a tablespoon or flat-bladed knife, scrape against the scales working from tail to head, to loosen and remove scales. Scaling the fish in this manner will prevent scales flicking all over the kitchen sink and walls.

To gut fish: slit the belly of the fish open. Remove the insides and wash the cavity clean with cold running water. Any blood can be removed by rubbing with a little salt.

COOKING FISH

Cooking fish is incredibly simple. Unfortunately, many people aren't sure what to do with fish, whether it is whole, in fillets or cutlets, but cooking fish is really quite easy when you follow a few rules:

- most important — do not overcook fish
- whole fish should be scored with 2 to 3 diagonal cuts across the body on both sides, to allow for even cooking
- fish is ready as soon as it loses its translucent appearance and turns opaque all the way through; overcooking spoils its flavour and texture
- use a moderate heat to prevent overcooking
- fish should be turned only once during cooking; turn half way through the cooking time
- to test fish for doneness, insert the tip of a knife into the thickest part of the flesh and gently divide it. It is cooked if it flakes easily. If you feel resistance as the knife cuts through, further cooking is required

As a guide, general cooking times for fish are as follows (for pan frying, grilling, barbecuing and shallow frying):

- fillets: 2 to 3 minutes per side
- cutlets: 3 to 4 minutes per side
- whole fish: 4 to 5 minutes per side

For microwaving fish:

- fillets: 500 g, 5 minutes on 70% power
- cutlets: 500 g, 6 minutes on 70% power
- whole fish: 1 kg, 10 minutes on 70% power

For baking fish:

- fillets, cutlets and whole fish: 20 minutes per kg

There are many methods to cook fish and some of these are listed below:

GRILLING Fillets, cutlets and whole fish are suitable for grilling. As grilling is a form of direct heat, marinating and basting the fish is recommended, as it will prevent it from drying. Fish should be placed under a preheated griller and cooked on a moderate heat.

Fish suitable for grilling include all oily fish: mullet, mackerel, sardines, tailor, blackfish; and moist fish including ling, shark, sea perch.

PAN FRYING Fillets, cutlets and whole fish are suitable for pan frying. Fish can be pan fried in a small amount of oil, or a mixture of oil and butter. Heat oil before cooking, so fish sizzles as it is added to the pan.

Fish may be coated in seasoned flour, breadcrumbs, polenta, rolled oats, shredded coconut or crushed savoury biscuits and many more. The coatings may be flavoured with chopped herbs, spices, chopped nuts, parmesan cheese or desiccated coconut.

STEAMING Fillets, cutlets and whole fish are suitable for steaming. Water should be boiling rapidly and should not touch the fish. Place seasoned fish in a steamer, with lid tightly closed. Cooking times vary for different fish, so cook until flesh flakes when tested with a fork.

Fish for steaming may be flavoured with strips of lemon, orange or lime rind, ginger, herbs, spices and chopped spring onions.

POACHING Fillets, cutlets and whole fish are suitable for poaching. Place fish in enough liquid to just cover and gently simmer. Do not allow the liquid to reach boiling point, as this will damage the flesh and overcook the fish. Fish is cooked when flesh flakes easily when tested with a fork.

Liquid for poaching may include a mixture of the following: water, stock, wine, court bouillon. These can be flavoured with lemon or orange slices, herbs, spices, ginger and vegetables.

The poaching liquid may be used as a base for a sauce. If fish is to be served cold, it may be left in the poaching liquid to cool. This will help fish to retain moisture and flavour.

BAKING Fillets, cutlets and whole fish are suitable for baking. Baking is especially suited to large whole fish. Place fish in a greased baking dish. Extra flavouring may be added, for example herbs, lemon or orange slices, stock or white wine. Cover the baking dish with foil or lid to retain moisture in the fish.

Unless a recipe states another temperature, baked fish is usually cooked at 190°C (375°F).

DEEP FRYING Fillets and very small whole fish are suitable for deep frying. Fish must be covered in some form of coating to protect it from overcooking. Coatings may be batters, breadcrumbs or seasoned flour. The coated fish is fully immersed in hot oil and cooked until the coating is brown and crispy. Do not overcrowd the pan, as this will lower the temperature of the oil, resulting in soggy fish. Remove from oil and drain on paper towelling. Fish may be kept warm in a preheated oven while cooking remaining fish.

MICROWAVING Fillets, cutlets and whole fish are suitable for microwaving. As long as fish is not overcooked in the microwave oven, the result is perfect — moist, tender fish with a pleasant fresh sea taste. When microwaving seafood, the following should be remembered:

- cover seafood loosely with cling wrap to allow steam to escape
- fish is cooking when it flakes easily at its thickest part

- shellfish is cooked when transparent flesh becomes white and shells on crustaceans turn orange-red in colour
- never cook live seafood — drown first in fresh water or freeze for 2 to 3 hours
- fold tail end of fillet under to give uniform depth
- arrange seafood with thickest section towards outside edge of dish
- arrange seafood in a single flat layer for faster and more uniform cooking
- pierce or remove eyes
- scallops, squid and cuttlefish which are high in moisture are best cooked in liquid or sauce, rather than butter or oil
- to remove fish odour from microwave oven, heat a bowl of water containing cut lemon slices on high for 6 to 8 minutes

BARBECUING Fillets, cutlets and whole fish are suitable for barbecuing. Fillets and cutlets should be marinated first, to add extra flavour and moisture. Whilst cooking, baste with marinade to prevent fish from drying out.

Fillets and cutlets should be placed on a well greased plate or grill, to avoid catching. Large whole fish is best wrapped in greased foil, with the cavity of the fish filled with herbs and lemon or orange slices for added flavour.

Do not place fish over an open flame. For best results, allow fire to burn down to a bed of glowing embers.

SEAFOOD
SCHOOL
Ph (02) 660 1611
FISH MARKETING AUTHORITY

Acknowledgements: special thanks to the Sydney Seafood School for the above information and for their advice and assistance in the preparation of this book.

FISH
from the
SEA

There are more than 20 000 species of fish in the seas of the world, so the possibilities of taste and flavour are endless. Recipes in this section use fish such as mullet, ocean perch, leatherjacket, snapper, sea bream, tailor, tuna and many more. For each recipe, several suggestions are given for suitable fish to use. For example hake, cod and haddock are interchangeable and can also be used instead of whiting and ling. It's also a good idea to ask your fishmonger for recommendations.

Fish as a main course is versatile, tasty and low in kilojoules, and of course it is renowned as the 'heart food' because of its cholesterol reducing properties. To keep the meal healthy, serve salad and lightly cooked vegetables.

You will find many delightful recipes for soups, pies and kebabs, and a multitude of ways to cook fish, including barbecuing, baking, stuffing, frying and grilling. Whichever method you choose, you can make a variety of dishes by using different sauces and herbs.

No seafood cookbook would be complete without a recipe for fish stock (see page 88). Every cook who likes seafood should have a ready supply of fish stock, an essential element in many recipes. Make large quantities of stock and keep frozen in small portions. It will keep in the refrigerator for 3 days.

FISHERMAN'S SOUP

500 g fish fillets (ling, cod, hake or gemfish)

2 large onions, thinly sliced

2 cloves garlic, chopped

350 g potatoes, sliced

1½ cups (375 ml) tomato purée

½ teaspoon coriander seeds, crushed

**4 cups (1 litre) Fish Stock
(see recipe page 88)**

freshly ground black pepper

400 g mussels, scrubbed and cleaned

125 g peeled green prawns (shrimps), deveined

1 Check fish fillets for bones and cut in half.

2 Cover the bottom of a flameproof casserole with onions, garlic and potatoes.

3 Combine tomato purée, coriander seeds and fish stock, and pour into casserole. Bring to the boil, reduce heat and simmer, covered, for 15 minutes or until potatoes are almost tender.

4 Add fish fillets and cook over a low heat for 4 minutes. Taste and adjust seasoning with pepper. Add mussels and prawns and continue cooking until the fish is tender and the mussels have opened. Discard any mussels that remain shut.

5 Serve with croutons that have been rubbed with garlic and fried in olive oil until crisp and golden.

SERVES 6

TURKISH FISH SOUP

**4 cups (1 litre) Fish Stock
(see recipe page 88)**

1 bay leaf

ground white pepper

3 tablespoons chopped fresh parsley

¼ teaspoon ground saffron threads

500 g white fish fillets

juice ½ to 1 lemon

3 egg yolks

extra chopped fresh parsley, to garnish

1 Bring fish stock, bay leaf, pepper, parsley and saffron to the boil. Reduce heat and simmer for 15 minutes, then strain and reheat.

2 While stock is simmering, check fillets for bones, cut crossways into 2.5 cm strips.

3 Add fish to simmering stock and poach for 5 minutes or until tender. Blend lemon juice with egg yolks and add ¼ cup (60 ml) of the hot liquid, whisking constantly. Return to the pan and heat gently. Serve hot sprinkled with parsley.

SERVES 4 TO 6

FISH CHOWDER

2 to 2.5 kg assorted whole fish (red mullet, ocean perch, leatherjacket)

8 cups (2 litres) water

2 lemons

4 tablespoons olive oil

2 onions, thinly sliced

2 cloves garlic, crushed

1 medium potato, diced

5 tomatoes, peeled and chopped

2 tablespoons finely chopped celery leaves

3 tablespoons dry white wine

1 bay leaf

salt

freshly ground black pepper

2 tablespoons chopped fresh parsley

1 Gut and fillet fish then skin fillets. Wash heads, bones and tails of fish. Place in a pan with water. Bring to the boil, reduce heat and simmer for 20 minutes. Drain well, reserving stock.

2 Check fillets for bones, cut into 5 cm serving pieces. Sprinkle with juice of 1 lemon.

3 Heat oil in a large saucepan, add onions and garlic and fry until onions are transparent. Add potato, tomatoes and celery leaves and cook over a low heat for 5 minutes.

4 Combine reserved stock and wine and add to tomato mixture with bay leaf. Bring to the boil, reduce heat and simmer, partially covered, for 40 minutes. Strain mixture and press vegetables through a sieve. There should be approximately 6 cups (1.5 litres) of liquid.

5 Bring liquid back to the boil. Add salt and pepper to taste, and parsley. Add fish and cook over a gentle heat until it flakes easily when tested. Taste and adjust flavouring with the remaining lemon juice.

SERVES 6 TO 8

POACHED FILLETS *in* DILL SAUCE

500 g ocean perch or gemfish fillets

2½ cups (625 ml) water

1 onion, sliced

1 small bay leaf

1 tablespoon butter

1 tablespoon plain flour

½ cup (125 ml) sour cream

2 tablespoons chopped fresh dill

ground white pepper

1 Check fillets for bones and wipe with a damp cloth.

2 Combine water, onion and bay leaf in a saucepan. Bring to the boil and reduce heat

to low. Slide in fish fillets and poach over a gentle heat for 5 minutes or until fillets flake easily when tested (about 10 minutes). Remove fish with a slotted spoon and keep warm on a serving dish.

3 Strain stock and reserve 1 cup (250 ml). Heat butter, add flour and cook for 2 minutes, stirring. Remove from heat and gradually add reserved stock, stirring constantly. Bring to the boil, reduce heat and simmer, stirring occasionally, until thickened.

4 Remove from heat and stir through sour cream and dill. Taste and adjust seasoning with white pepper. Spoon sauce over fish and serve hot.

SERVES 4

Poached Fillets in Dill Sauce

Stuffed Fish

STUFFED FISH

1 kg whole fish (snapper, sea bream or tailor), gutted and scaled

salt

juice 1 lemon

30 g butter

STUFFING

2 tablespoons olive oil

1 small onion, finely chopped

3 tablespoons chopped celery leaves

2 tablespoons chopped fresh parsley

1 cup (60 g) fresh breadcrumbs

salt

freshly ground black pepper

juice ½ lemon

1 egg, beaten

SAUCE

1 tablespoon olive oil

1 onion, finely chopped

1 green capsicum (pepper), sliced

4 tomatoes, peeled and chopped

pinch cayenne pepper

juice ½ lemon

2 tablespoons chopped fresh parsley

1 Preheat oven to 180°C (350°F).

2 Clean fish, season with salt and sprinkle with lemon juice. Set aside.

3 TO PREPARE STUFFING: Heat oil in a pan and sauté onion for 2 minutes. Add celery leaves and parsley and cook for a further 2 minutes. Stir through breadcrumbs and season with salt, pepper and lemon juice. Cool for a few minutes and stir in egg.

4 Place stuffing in cavity of fish and secure the opening with skewers. Place fish in a greased baking dish and dot with butter. Bake in oven for 30 to 35 minutes or until fish flakes easily when tested.

5 To Prepare Sauce: Heat oil in a pan and sauté onion for 2 minutes. Add capsicum (pepper) and tomatoes and cook for a further 3 minutes. Stir through cayenne, lemon juice and 2 tablespoons water. Bring to the boil, reduce heat and simmer until sauce is thick. Stir in parsley.

6 When the fish is cooked remove to a serving dish and pour sauce over. Serve hot with boiled rice.

Serves 4

Fish Pie

60 g butter

¼ cup (30 g) plain flour

2½ cups (625 ml) milk

375 g cooked white fish (trevally, redfish or kingfish), flaked

100 g cooked royal red prawns (shrimps)

100 g scallops

juice ½ lemon

salt and pepper

500 g potatoes, cooked

extra butter and milk

1 egg, beaten

1 Preheat oven to 180°C (350°F).

2 Heat butter in a pan, add flour and cook for 2 minutes. Gradually add milk off the heat then bring to the boil. Reduce heat and simmer for 5 minutes.

3 Off the heat stir through seafood, lemon juice and salt and pepper to taste. Cook over a gentle heat for 5 minutes or until heated through. Spoon fish mixture into an ovenproof dish.

4 Mash potatoes with butter and milk. Carefully smooth potato over fish. Decorate the surface with a fork and brush with egg. Cook in oven until golden. Serve hot with peas and garnish with fresh mint.

Serves 4 to 6

Fish Kebabs

750 g firm fish fillets (kingfish, silver warehou or tuna), cut into 6 cm squares

Marinade

½ cup (125 ml) oil

½ cup (125 ml) fresh lemon juice

½ cup (125 ml) dry white wine

salt and pepper

chopped fresh rosemary or basil

1 Combine marinade ingredients, pour over fish pieces and leave to marinate for at least 2 hours in refrigerator.

2 Thread fish pieces on skewers when required and cook over barbecue coals, basting occasionally with remaining marinade.

Serves 4

Fish Pie

FISH AND CHIPS

This famous English dish needs no introduction. Choose fillets that are the same thickness so that they cook evenly. The secret to producing good chips is double frying, that is cooking the chips until almost tender then draining well and refrying. The traditional accompaniment to hot fish and chips is brown vinegar.

FISH *and* CHIPS

750 g fish fillets (flathead, ling or hake)

1 tablespoon fresh lemon juice

½ cup (60 g) plain flour

BATTER

1 cup (125 g) plain flour

½ teaspoon baking powder

salt and pepper

1 cup (250 ml) milk

CHIPS

3 large potatoes, peeled and sliced

oil for deep frying

1 Check fish fillets for bones. Sprinkle with the lemon juice.

2 TO PREPARE BATTER: Sift flour, baking powder, salt and pepper into a bowl. Make a well in the centre and pour in milk. Stirring from the centre, gradually incorporate flour. Keep stirring until all flour is incorporated then beat well. If batter is still lumpy, whisk or sieve it.

3 TO PREPARE CHIPS: Cut potato slices into chips. Place in a bowl of iced water for 5 minutes. Drain well and pat chips dry. Heat oil to 190°C (375°F). Place chips in a frying basket and lower into oil. Cook chips until almost tender and drain well.

4 Dredge fish fillets with flour and pat off any excess. Dip fish into batter to coat. Fry fish in chip oil for 5 minutes. Drain well. Reheat oil to 190°C (375°F) and refry until fish is tender and batter is golden and crisp. Drain well and keep warm.

5 Reheat oil to 190°C (375°F). Fry chips for 3 to 4 minutes or until crisp and golden. Drain well and serve hot with fish.

SERVES 4

BAKED FISH *with* TOMATOES

1.5 kg whole fish, gutted (jewfish, silver bream or snapper), scaled and cleaned

salt and black pepper

juice 1 lemon

SAUCE

5 tablespoons olive oil

1 large onion, sliced

2 cloves garlic, crushed

4 tomatoes, skinned and sliced

⅓ cup (80 ml) white wine

⅓ cup finely chopped fresh parsley

1 Preheat oven to 190°C (375°F).

2 Season fish with salt and pepper. Sprinkle with lemon juice and allow to stand for 30 minutes.

3 TO PREPARE SAUCE: Heat oil in a pan and cook onion until translucent. Add garlic and cook for a further 3 minutes.

4 Add tomatoes and wine. Season with salt and pepper to taste. Simmer for 10 minutes. Stir through parsley.

5 Place fish in a lightly greased baking dish and pour over the sauce. Bake for 30 to 40 minutes or until the fish flakes easily when tested. Serve with crusty bread and cabbage salad.

SERVES 4

FISH IN BEER BATTER

This can be used to deep fry all seafood. To make the batter, sift 2 cups (250 g) plain flour with a pinch of salt. Mix ⅔ cup (150 ml) flat beer (lager) and an egg yolk with ⅔ cup (150 ml) milk and blend into flour to form smooth batter. Beat 2 egg whites to soft peaks. Fold into batter with 1½ tablespoons oil. Coat fish with flour and deep fry in oil heated to 190°C (375°F).

STEP-BY-STEP TECHNIQUES

FISH ROLL *with* CHEESE SAUCE

1 packet (375 g) frozen puff pastry, thawed

3 tablespoons gherkin relish

1 tablespoon grated onion

500 g white fish fillets (mirror dory, gemfish, kingfish, hake or trevally), cooked and flaked

1½ tablespoons chopped fresh parsley

salt and pepper to taste

1 egg, beaten

extra fresh parsley, to garnish

CHEESE SAUCE

2 tablespoons butter

2 tablespoons plain flour

1½ cups (375 ml) milk

½ cup (60 g) grated sharp Cheddar cheese

pinch cayenne pepper

salt and pepper

1 Preheat oven to 230°C (450°F).

2 Roll pastry out on a floured surface to a 30 cm x 35 cm rectangle. Spread with gherkin relish, onion and fish, leaving 1 cm margin all round. Sprinkle with parsley and seasoning.

3 Roll up like a Swiss roll, place on a greased oven tray and brush with beaten egg. Bake for 15 minutes. Reduce heat slightly and bake a further 15 minutes or until pastry is cooked through. Serve with cheese sauce, garnished with parsley sprigs.

4 TO PREPARE SAUCE: Melt butter, stir in flour and cook for 1 minute without letting it brown. Gradually stir in milk and bring to the boil. Remove from heat, add cheese and stir until melted. Add cayenne pepper. Season to taste.

SERVES 4

Spread onion, fish and gherkin over pastry. Sprinkle parsley over fish.

Roll up like a Swiss roll.

Fish Roll with Cheese Sauce

FENNEL

Fennel has a similar flavour to aniseed. It is available in autumn, winter and spring. Buy fennel that is crisp and well shaped, make sure it does not have withered stalks. Store it in the refrigerator in a plastic bag.

FISH BARBECUED *with* FENNEL

4 medium white-fleshed whole fish (silver bream, mullet, tailor or hake)

1 large bunch fennel

MARINADE

½ cup (125 ml) olive oil

juice 1 lemon

4 tablespoons cognac or brandy

salt and freshly ground black pepper

2 cloves garlic, crushed

1 Scale, gut and clean fish. Place one fennel branch inside each fish. Score fish with three 5 cm long incisions in each side.

2 Combine marinade ingredients, pour over fish and marinate 1 hour in foil.

3 Place remaining fennel stalks in oven at 100°C (200°F) until dried out. Transfer dried fennel to the barbecue over hot coals. Barbecue fish over fennel for 5 minutes each side or until the fish flakes easily when tested. The fennel will burn, imparting an aromatic taste to the fish.

SERVES 4

DEVILLED FISH

750 g lean fish fillets (blackfish, trevally, redfish or hake)

Court Bouillon (see recipe page 88)

1 medium onion, finely chopped

2½ tablespoons butter

2½ tablespoons plain flour

¼ teaspoon cayenne pepper

¼ teaspoon dry mustard

1 tablespoon chopped fresh parsley

3 teaspoons Worcestershire sauce

salt and pepper to taste

4 egg yolks

1 cup (60 g) soft breadcrumbs

extra butter

parsley-tipped lemon wedges

1 Preheat oven to 180°C (350°F).

2 Poach fish in court bouillon for 5 minutes or until flesh flakes easily. Drain and flake, reserving 1½ cups (375 ml) stock.

3 Sauté onion in butter until soft. Add flour and cook, stirring for 2 minutes. Do not allow to brown. Gradually stir in stock. Bring to the boil and cook gently for a few minutes. Add cayenne, mustard, parsley and Worcestershire sauce. Season to taste.

4 Stir 2 tablespoons hot liquid into beaten yolks and return to pan. Stir in fish. Divide between 4 ovenproof dishes. Sprinkle with breadcrumbs, dot with butter and bake for 15 minutes. Garnish with lemon wedges.

SERVES 4

FRESH TUNA ALGARVE STYLE

4 tuna steaks

2 tablespoons olive oil

2 cloves garlic, crushed

MARINADE

½ cup (125 ml) dry white wine

2 tablespoons fresh lemon juice

salt and ground black pepper

2 sprigs parsley

1 Place tuna in a bowl. Combine marinade ingredients. Pour over fish and marinate for 4 to 8 hours, turning occasionally. Drain fish, pat dry and reserve marinade.

2 Heat oil in a pan and cook garlic for 2 minutes on low heat. Fry fish for about 12 minutes, turning after 6 minutes, or until tender.

3 Pour in marinade and heat through. Remove parsley. Serve with boiled potatoes and spinach.

SERVES 4

Fresh Tuna Algarve Style

Each region in Italy has its own version of fish stew or bouillabaisse, often made with the less expensive varieties of fish. It should always include two or more kinds of squid and some crustaceans, as well as a selection of fish in season. This dish can also be prepared in advance and reheated.

ITALIAN FISH STEW

1 kg mixed fish (prawns/shrimps, calamari/squid, cuttlefish, mussels, whiting, redfish, leatherjacket, etc.)

2 cups (500 ml) olive oil

½ cup (125 ml) white wine

2 onions, sliced

2 cloves garlic, crushed

2 tablespoons chopped fresh parsley

2 tablespoons tomato paste

2 tablespoons white wine vinegar

salt and pepper

1 Clean and scale fish and cut in pieces if too big. Shell seafood. Slice calamari and cuttlefish into rings.

2 Warm oil in a heavy saucepan. If using cuttlefish, put it in the pan first, as it takes longer to cook, and sauté for about 10 minutes depending on size. Then add all fish and calamari, keeping prawns and mussels for later.

3 Add wine and continue to cook on a slow heat. When the fish looks nearly cooked, add the shellfish and simmer for a further 2 minutes. With a slotted spoon, lift out all fish and shellfish and put in a bowl or plate.

4 To the remaining juices in the pan add onions, garlic and parsley and cook for a few minutes.

5 Add tomato paste and ¾ cup (180 ml) warm water and simmer for 40 minutes.

6 Add fish and vinegar, season to taste with salt and pepper and continue cooking for another 10 minutes. Serve immediately.

SERVES 4

CRISPY FISH PIE

375 g white fish fillets (mullet, hairtail or flathead), cut into 2.5 cm strips

1 large onion, sliced

⅔ cup (150 ml) milk

2 tablespoons butter or margarine

3 tablespoons plain flour

¾ cup (90 g) grated cheese

3 large tomatoes, peeled and sliced

½ cup (30 g) fresh breadcrumbs

1 Preheat oven to 190°C (375°F).

2 Place fish in a greased ovenproof dish and season. Arrange onion slices over the top and pour over milk. Cover and bake for 40 minutes. Remove.

3 Melt butter in a pan. Stir in flour and cook for 2 to 3 minutes, stirring all the time. Spoon liquid from cooked fish into a pan. Bring to the boil, stirring constantly, and cook 2 to 3 minutes. Remove pan from heat and stir in two thirds of the cheese.

4 Arrange tomatoes over fish and pour over the sauce. Sprinkle breadcrumbs on top with remaining cheese. Return dish to oven for 10 to 15 minutes until golden.

SERVES 4

SPICY MARINATED MULLET

750 g mullet fillets

MARINADE

1 medium onion, finely chopped

2 cm piece fresh ginger, finely grated

1 clove garlic, crushed

3 tablespoons cider vinegar

3 tablespoons dry sherry

3 drops Tabasco sauce

1 Combine the marinade ingredients in a bowl, mixing well.

2 Lay fillets into a shallow dish and pour the marinade over. Cover and place in the refrigerator for approximately 2 hours.

3 Prepare barbecue to a medium heat and oil the plate or grill. Place fillets over heat and cook for approximately 3 minutes each side. Turn only once during cooking.

4 Serve with foiled barbecue potatoes and cucumber salad.

SERVES 4

FILLETS *in* HONEY MARINADE

500 g fish fillets (ling, hake or cod)

fresh coriander, to garnish

MARINADE

3 tablespoons honey

1 tablespoon orange rind, cut into strips and blanched

1 teaspoon teriyaki sauce (soy sauce can be substituted)

¼ teaspoon chilli powder

1 teaspoon freshly grated ginger

1 tablespoon fresh orange juice

3 spring onions, thinly sliced

ground black pepper

1 Combine marinade ingredients in a saucepan. Heat gently, enough for honey to melt.

2 Cut the fillets into serving size portions. 'Score' (cut the flesh two or three times with a knife) each piece and place in a dish. Cover with the marinade and allow to stand for 1 to 2 hours in refrigerator.

3 Place fish pieces onto a lightly oiled barbecue plate or grill. Cook on medium heat for approximately 3 minutes each side. During cooking baste generously with marinade.

4 To serve, pour remaining marinade over fish. Serve with fluffy white rice and garnish with fresh coriander.

SERVES 4

FISH *with* OLIVES

1 to 1.5 kg whole snapper (or silver bream or ocean perch)

plain flour

⅓ cup (80 ml) olive oil

2 cloves garlic, crushed

1 tablespoon white wine vinegar

salt and pepper

200 g black olives, stoned

1 Clean, scale, wash and dry fish carefully. Season lightly and coat with flour. Shake off excess.

2 In a wide pan, heat olive oil, and when it starts to smoke, add fish and fry at high heat for a couple of minutes on each side to seal the skin.

3 Lower heat, add garlic, vinegar and seasoning and cover it with a lid. When fish looks nearly cooked (the eye will look like a white pearl) add olives and shake the pan, so that the flavour of the olives penetrates the fish.

4 To serve, arrange snapper on a heated serving dish, decorate with olives, and pour cooking juices over it.

SERVES 4

 READY-TO-USE GARLIC

Garlic is required in many recipes so it's useful to have some ready to use, to save time. Crushed garlic can be bought in jars in supermarkets however this is quite expensive. You can make your own very easily and cheaply. Place several cloves of garlic in the food processor, with a little white vinegar and blend. Store in the refrigerator in an airtight jar and use whenever crushed garlic is required in a recipe.

TOMATO PASTA *with* FISH *and* HORSERADISH

salt

juice 1 large lemon

1 small carrot, 1 celery stalk and 1 parsley sprig, tied together

600 g fish fillets (ling, sea perch, gemfish or hake)

500 g fresh tomato pasta (tagliatelle or spirelli)

2 tablespoons grated horseradish root

1 tablespoon plain flour

1⅔ cups (400 ml) sour cream

30 g butter

1 teaspoon chopped fresh dill, plus few sprigs for decoration

1 In a large saucepan of cold water put some salt, lemon juice and the vegetables and bring to the boil.

2 Add fish and gently simmer until cooked through. Remove with a slotted spoon and set aside; discard vegetables.

3 When fish has cooled slightly, cut into large serving pieces and keep warm. Bring the cooking water back to the boil, add pasta and cook until 'al dente'.

4 In a small saucepan heat horseradish. Sprinkle flour over it and stir over a low heat until the flour browns slightly. Add sour cream and heat through; do not boil. Add butter and stir until it melts, then whisk in 1 tablespoon pasta cooking water and the chopped dill.

5 Drain the cooked pasta and transfer to a warm serving plate. Top with fish pieces, pour sauce over the top and add the sprigs of dill before serving immediately.

SERVES 4

FISH FILLETS *with* EGGPLANT

8 fish fillets (sea bream, mirror dory or sand whiting)

oil

1 lemon

salt and pepper

1 large eggplant (aubergine), cut lengthways in 8 slices, 1 cm thick

plain flour

1 egg, beaten

50 g butter

GARLIC BUTTER

100 g butter

3 to 4 cloves garlic, crushed

1 Marinate the fish fillets for 30 minutes or more in a little oil, lemon, salt and pepper, turning occasionally.

2 Coat eggplant slices with flour and egg and fry them in butter until golden.

3 TO PREPARE GARLIC BUTTER: Cream butter and crushed garlic cloves.

4 Grill the fish fillets, and rest each one on a slice of eggplant. Decorate each fillet with garlic butter.

SERVES 4

 EGGPLANT (AUBERGINE)

Choose eggplants which are firm and smooth and have no spots. They can be stored unwrapped in the refrigerator for about two weeks. Eggplant can have a bitter taste so it is often best to sprinkle it with salt and leave for 15 minutes for the bitter juices to be extracted. Then rinse thoroughly, pat dry and use immediately. Eggplant can be fried, grilled, stuffed, marinated and used in casseroles.

COLD MARINATED FISH

800 g small fish fillets (red mullet, redfish, red spot whiting or ocean perch)

plain flour

⅓ cup (80 ml) olive oil

4 white onions, thinly sliced

1 sprig rosemary

1 bay leaf, crumbled

2 tablespoons white wine vinegar

1 lemon rind, grated

1 Cover fillets in flour, then shallow fry in half the oil. Drain and arrange in a dish.

2 Add the rest of the oil to the pan together with onions, rosemary and bay leaf and cook gently.

3 When onion is cooked, but not brown, add vinegar and 2 tablespoons of water and let it evaporate to half its quantity. Mix through lemon rind. Pour this marinade on the cooked fillets and refrigerate for a day before serving. Serve with hot crusty bread to soak up the juices.

SERVES 4

BREAM *with* OYSTER STUFFING

1 to 2 kg whole bream (or snapper or jewfish)

4 tablespoons butter

1 tablespoon fresh lemon juice

3 bacon rashers

STUFFING

1½ tablespoons chopped onion

3 tablespoons chopped celery

2 tablespoons butter

1 small jar oysters, drained

1½ cups stale bread cubes

1 tablespoon chopped fresh parsley

salt and pepper

evaporated milk

Add evaporated milk to moisten.

Spoon stuffing into fish cavity.

1 Preheat oven to 180°C (350°F).

2 TO PREPARE STUFFING: Sauté onion and celery in butter until soft. Add oysters and cook 1 minute. Mix with bread cubes, parsley, salt and pepper and enough evaporated milk to moisten.

3 Fill fish cavity with this mixture. Secure with toothpicks. Place in greased baking dish, brush with butter and lemon juice and top with bacon rashers. Bake for 50 minutes. Serve with creamed potatoes.

SERVES 6

Bream with Oyster Stuffing

BREAM *with* WHITE WINE *and* MUSHROOMS

4 x 185 g bream fillets (or barramundi or whiting)

2 spring onions, chopped

250 g button mushrooms, sliced

1¾ cups (450 ml) Fish Stock (see recipe page 88)

1 egg yolk

⅔ cup (150 ml) cream

1 teaspoon cornflour

salt and pepper

juice 1 lemon

30 g butter

1 tablespoon chopped fresh parsley

extra parsley, to garnish

1 Wipe fillets and check for bones.

2 Place in a lightly greased flameproof casserole dish and sprinkle with spring onions and half the mushrooms. Pour over stock and bake in oven for 15 minutes at 190°C (375°F) or until fish flakes easily.

3 Drain fish fillets, reserving liquid, place on a serving dish and keep warm.

4 Combine egg yolk, cream and cornflour. Reduce cooking liquid and gradually add cream mixture. Cook over gentle heat until thickened slightly. Taste and adjust seasoning and add lemon juice.

5 In another pan, cook remaining mushrooms in butter until soft. Add parsley and stir through. Pour sauce over fillets and arrange mushrooms around. Garnish with parsley. Serve hot with rice.

SERVES 4

Bream with White Wine and Mushrooms

WHITING LASAGNE ROLLS NEAPOLITAN

2 teaspoons olive oil

12 sheets green lasagne

12 whiting fillets (or mirror dory, ling or hake)

½ teaspoon dried basil

salt

freshly ground black pepper

4 tablespoons Parmesan cheese

4 large tomatoes, peeled and chopped

1 onion, finely chopped

2 tablespoons chopped fresh parsley

1 tablespoon oil

1 clove garlic, crushed

½ red capsicum (pepper), sliced

1 Preheat oven to 200°C (400°F).

2 Cook lasagne sheets one at a time in boiling, salted water with olive oil. The saucepan should be about two-thirds full. Cook each sheet for 2 minutes (after the water has returned to the boil) then remove lasagne and drain. Continue in this way until all are cooked.

3 Gently simmer fillets in 1 cup (250 ml) water with basil, salt and pepper for 5 minutes. Remove the fish and place one fillet on each sheet of lasagne, sprinkling with Parmesan cheese. Roll up each one and place, seams down, in an ovenproof dish and set aside.

4 Combine tomatoes, onion, parsley, oil, garlic and capsicum, in a pan over high heat, then simmer for 10 minutes. Spoon sauce over the rolls and bake for 15 minutes. Serve two rolls per portion with the sauce.

SERVES 6

COLD FISH *with* OIL AND LEMON

1 to 1.5 kg whole snapper (or silver bream or leatherjacket), cleaned and scaled

parsley sprigs, to garnish

COURT BOUILLON

1 carrot, sliced

1 onion, sliced

1 celery stalk, sliced

1 bay leaf

6 peppercorns

SAUCE

⅓ cup (80 ml) olive oil

juice 3 lemons

salt and pepper

3 tablespoons chopped fresh parsley

1 TO PREPARE COURT BOUILLON: Simmer for 30 minutes the carrot, onion, celery, bay leaf and peppercorns in slightly salted water (enough to cover the fish).

2 Simmer the fish in the court bouillon until just cooked and allow to cool in its own liquid.

3 TO PREPARE SAUCE: Combine oil, lemon juice, salt and pepper to taste, and parsley.

4 Drain the fish and arrange on a serving platter. Decorate it with sprigs of parsley and pour half the sauce on top. Serve the rest of the sauce separately. If you prefer, fish prepared this way is also good with a homemade mayonnaise.

SERVES 4

 HOMEMADE MAYONNAISE

Make your own mayonnaise by mixing an egg yolk with 1 teaspoon mustard, and whisk in 1 cup (250 ml) oil. When the mixture is thick, add salt, pepper and 1 teaspoon white vinegar.

Italian Bream

Italian Bream

1.5 kg whole bream (sea bream, silver bream or whiting), gutted

250 g mussels, scrubbed and beards removed

2 tomatoes, peeled and chopped

1 teaspoon tomato paste

1 teaspoon chopped fresh chervil or good pinch dried chervil

10 black olives

Marinade

1¼ cups (300 ml) dry white wine

⅔ cup (150 ml) water

1 onion, thickly sliced

1 bouquet garni

6 black peppercorns

1 Preheat oven to 180°C (350°F).

2 Clean fish and check for scales.

3 **To Prepare Marinade:** Combine wine, water, onion, bouquet garni and peppercorns in a saucepan. Bring to the boil and simmer for 3 minutes. Pour over the fish and marinate for 3 hours.

4 Place fish in a shallow ovenproof dish. Separately, bring marinade to the boil, add mussels and cook, covered, for 5 minutes. Strain mussels, reserving liquid. Discard mussels that have not opened. Remove mussels from shells.

5 Stir tomatoes and paste into marinade. Taste and adjust seasoning and add chervil. Pour around fish and add olives. Bake for 25 to 30 minutes or until the fish flakes when tested. Garnish with mussels.

Serves 4

 Bouquet Garni

Classic bouquet garni is made up from marjoram, parsley, thyme and bay leaves, and sometimes peppercorns. These are tied up in a piece of muslin. It is used to flavour soups, stews and casseroles. Bouquet garni can be bought ready-made from supermarkets.

POACHED SNAPPER

1 kg whole snapper (or leatherjacket or sea
bream), gutted and scaled

4 tomatoes, skinned, seeded and chopped

1 onion, finely chopped

4 spring onions, finely sliced

2 tablespoons chopped fresh parsley

1¼ cups (300 ml) Fish Stock
(see recipe page 88)

60 g butter

salt and pepper

1 tablespoon plain flour

1 Preheat oven to 190°C (375°F).

2 Wipe fish and clean backbone. If
snapper is large, cut into steaks, otherwise
leave whole.

3 Lightly grease a baking dish with butter
and arrange half the tomatoes, onion and
spring onions on base. Place fish on
vegetables and cover with remaining
vegetables. Sprinkle with half the parsley
then pour in stock. Dot the fish with 30 g
of butter.

4 Cook in oven for 30 minutes or until fish
flakes easily when tested.

5 Carefully lift fish to a serving dish and
keep warm. Pour cooking liquid and
vegetables into a small pan. Taste and adjust
seasoning. Bring to the boil and simmer
until reduced by a quarter.

6 Combine remaining butter with flour.
Gradually add mixture to pan and simmer
until sauce is thickened.

7 Taste and adjust seasoning and pour over
fish. Garnish with remaining parsley. Serve
with glazed carrots garnished with mustard
seeds and sautéed zucchini (courgettes)
garnished with caraway seeds.

SERVES 4

BAKED SNAPPER *with* CITRUS AND CORIANDER SAUCE

200 g penne pasta

½ cup (125 ml) vegetable oil

4 small-medium snapper steaks (or gemfish,
kingfish or blue eye cod), trimmed

2 to 3 cloves garlic, crushed

1 tablespoon chopped fresh coriander, and
some sprigs for decoration

⅔ cup (150 ml) tomato purée or juice from
canned, peeled tomatoes

3 tablespoons fresh citrus juice: lime, lemon,
Seville orange or a combination

chilli flakes, to taste

1 Preheat oven to 220°C (425°F).

2 Cook penne in boiling salted water until
barely 'al dente'. Drain, and stir through a
little vegetable oil to prevent sticking.
Transfer to an ovenproof dish.

3 In a pan, heat some of the oil and brown
the snapper on both sides. Transfer to the
dish and lay side by side on top of the penne,
covering it completely.

4 Heat remaining oil in pan and gently
sauté garlic. Add chopped coriander, tomato
purée and citrus juice. Cook, stirring, until
the sauce boils and gives off a citrus aroma.
Sprinkle in chilli flakes to taste, then pour
sauce over snapper. Pour in a little water,
(about 3 tablespoons), to make sure all the
pasta is moistened.

5 Cover loosely with foil and bake for
25 to 30 minutes, or until the snapper is
tender. Decorate with coriander sprigs and
serve from the dish.

SERVES 4

SNAPPER BAKED *in* WINE SAUCE

1.5 kg whole snapper (or bream, ocean perch or whiting)

1 teaspoon salt

freshly ground black pepper

1½ cups (375 ml) dry white wine

1 cup (250 ml) water

3 teaspoons mild French mustard

1½ tablespoons butter, melted

1 Preheat oven to 180°C (350°F).

2 Sprinkle fish inside and out with salt and pepper and place in an oiled baking dish. Combine wine, water and mustard and pour over fish.

3 Bake for 40 minutes, basting occasionally with the liquid. Pour melted butter over fish and serve hot.

SERVES 6

FISH IN A PAPER CASE

This is an ideal way to cook the more delicate fish as it preserves all the flavour. Serve the fish in its paper case and do the unwrapping at the table.

FISH *in a* PAPER CASE

25 g dried mushrooms or 150 g button mushrooms, chopped

25 g butter

1 clove garlic, crushed

2 tablespoons chopped fresh parsley

50 g prosciutto or bacon

1 to 1.5 kg whole snapper (or ocean perch, whiting or snapper)

salt and pepper

oil

1 Preheat oven to 180°C (350°F).

2 Soak the mushrooms in a little warm water, drain, chop and sauté in the butter with garlic. Add a couple of tablespoons of the water in which you have soaked the mushrooms and cook slowly for a few minutes.

3 Add parsley and prosciutto or bacon in thin strips, remove from heat and set aside.

4 Clean the fish, season it with salt, pepper and oil and arrange it on a sheet of greaseproof paper. Put the mushroom and prosciutto mixture on top and seal the paper so that it forms a bag from which no juices can escape.

5 Place fish in oven and cook for about 30 minutes.

6 Serve with sautéed button mushrooms and a fresh salad. You might also need some bread to soak up the delicious juices which will have formed.

SERVES 4

Arrange mixture on top of the cleaned fish.

Fold paper to make a sealed bag.

SNAPPER QUENELLES

**500 g snapper fillets
(or pike or sole)**

salt and white pepper

2 egg whites

1¼ cups (300 ml) cream, well chilled

**3 cups (750 ml) Fish Stock
(see recipe page 88)**

Nantua Sauce (see recipe page 89)

1 Skin snapper fillets and remove all bones.

2 Purée fish in a blender or food processor. Do not overprocess. For a finer quenelle, put flesh through a drum sieve. Season lightly with salt and pepper, cover and chill in refrigerator for 1 hour.

3 Whisk egg whites lightly until broken down but not frothy. Gradually add egg white to the fish, a teaspoon at a time, and beat well between additions. Chill mixture, covered, for a further 30 minutes.

4 Gradually add cream to mixture, whisking to incorporate. Return to refrigerator for a further 30 minutes.

5 Place Fish Stock in a frying pan and bring to the boil. Reduce heat and allow to simmer.

6 Using two wet tablespoons, shape fish mixture into ovals. Very carefully place in the stock and poach for 10 to 12 minutes or until cooked when tested. Using a slotted spoon, lift quenelles out of the stock and place on absorbent paper (paper towel) to dry. Remove to serving plate and serve hot with Nantua Sauce.

SERVES 6

SNAPPER QUENELLES

This dish requires great care, but is worth the effort.

Snapper Quenelles

Clean anchovies and remove the backbone.

Coat anchovies first with egg and then breadcrumbs.

Fry in butter until golden.

 ANCHOVY SAUCE

Roughly blend the yolks of three hard-boiled eggs with four anchovy fillets. Add oil and white wine vinegar to taste. Use the finely chopped whites for decoration.

FRESH ANCHOVY CUTLETS

**800 g fresh anchovies
(or sardines, garfish or red spot whiting)**

2 eggs

salt

breadcrumbs

150 g butter

1 To clean the anchovies or sardines, pull their heads off together with the intestines. Scrape off any scales with your fingers and wash the fish briefly. Open them to remove the backbone. Wash them briefly and dry carefully with absorbent paper.

2 Beat the eggs with the salt, and coat the anchovies first with egg mixture and then breadcrumbs. Fry them slowly in the butter until golden. Serve with anchovy sauce.

SERVES 4

FRESH ANCHOVIES *with* FENNEL SEEDS

800 g fresh anchovies (or sardines, silver biddies or garfish)

2 cups (500 ml) olive oil

2 cloves garlic, chopped

1 teaspoon fennel seeds

salt

1 Clean anchovies as above.

2 In a wide pan or a frying pan with lid, cook the oil and garlic on low heat, not allowing the garlic to brown. As soon as the oil is warm put in the anchovies and the fennel seeds. Season with a little salt. Cook very slowly for 15 minutes, checking from time to time that they are not sticking to the bottom of the pan. Serve with toasted slices of crusty bread.

SERVES 4

SPAGHETTI *with* ANCHOVIES *and* CAPERS

40 g butter

olive oil

2 cloves garlic, thinly sliced

4 anchovy fillets (or sardines, redfish or trevally), chopped

150 g black olives, stoned and chopped

1 tablespoon capers, chopped

4 tomatoes, peeled and chopped

salt and pepper

400 g spaghetti

1 tablespoon chopped fresh parsley

1 In a saucepan, warm the butter with a little oil and sauté garlic, anchovies, olives, capers and tomatoes. Cook slowly for 15 minutes, and season to taste.

2 Boil the spaghetti in plenty of water, drain and arrange on a serving plate. Pour the sauce on top and sprinkle with chopped parsley. Serve immediately.

SERVES 4

GRILLED SARDINES *in* MUSTARD SAUCE

24 fresh sardines (or garfish or red spot whiting), scaled, boned and gutted

rock (sea) salt, ground

75 g butter

1½ tablespoons plain flour

1⅓ cups (330 ml) dry white wine

2 tablespoons Dijon-style mustard

ground black pepper

juice 1 lemon

½ cup (30 g) fresh breadcrumbs

1 tablespoon chopped fresh parsley

1 Preheat oven to 210°C (425°F).

2 Cut through backbone of each sardine near the tail and remove backbone with as many other bones as possible.

3 Sprinkle sardines with rock salt and place under moderately hot griller for 2 to 3 minutes each side. Place in shallow ovenproof dish.

4 Melt 30 g butter, stir in flour and cook, stirring for 2 minutes. Remove from heat and gradually blend in wine. Return to heat and simmer for 3 minutes, stirring continuously. Add mustard, pepper and lemon juice. Pour sauce over fish.

5 Heat remaining butter and sauté breadcrumbs until golden brown. Sprinkle over fish and bake for 5 minutes. Serve sprinkled with parsley.

SERVES 4 TO 6

CAPERS

Capers are the unopened flower buds of a plant that grows in the Mediterranean. They are always sold in jars, pickled in wine vinegar and once opened should be stored in the refrigerator.

Grilled Sardines in Mustard Sauce

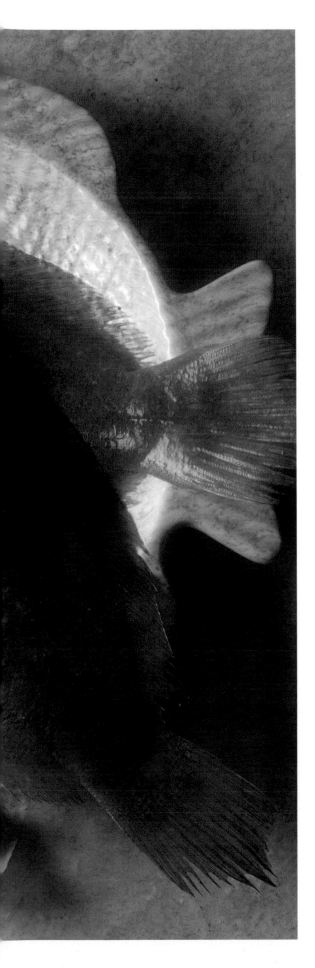

FLATFISH
from the sea

There are about 600 species of flatfish, the carnivorous bottom dwellers of the sea — they are bony, oval-shaped and flattened. The most common ones used are flounder, plaice, halibut, turbot and sole.

Flatfish can be purchased and served whole. Larger flatfish can be filleted and because of their shape, yield four fillets not two. Fillets may be small though so allow two to three per person.

Flatfish have a fine bone structure and soft white flesh with a mild taste. Sole and flounder are very popular and are available all year. Plaice and John Dory can be substituted.

As the flesh of flatfish is fine, gentle methods of cooking need to be used such as light grilling, baking, poaching and pan frying, and care should be taken not to overcook them. Whole fish can be stuffed with shellfish or breadcrumb and herb-based stuffings. Fillets can be stuffed, rolled and poached. Stuffings can usually be prepared a day in advance so you can save time when you need to prepare the meal. Sauces that go well with flatfish include white wine sauce, tartare sauce, crème fraîche and dill sauce.

Although there are several stages in the preparation of this dish, some stages can be prepared in advance. The stock, stuffing and both sauces can be prepared the day before. Bring velouté sauce to room temperature before coating fillets.

Note: Quantities can easily be doubled to turn this into a main dish.

FRIED STUFFED FILLETS *of* SOLE

4 fillets flounder or sole, skinned

salt and freshly ground pepper

½ cup (125 ml) white wine

⅔ cup (150 ml) Fish Stock (see recipe page 88)

1 tablespoon butter

1 tablespoon plain flour

finely grated nutmeg to taste

1 egg yolk

2 tablespoons sour cream

2 tablespoons oil

oil for deep-frying

1 cup (60 g) dried breadcrumbs

Fresh Tomato Sauce (see recipe page 91)

fresh parsley, to garnish

STUFFING

15 g butter

4 button mushrooms, finely chopped

1 spring onion, finely chopped

½ cup (30 g) fresh white breadcrumbs

1 Preheat oven to 200°C (400°F).

2 Wipe fillets, check for bones and season lightly with salt and pepper.

3 TO PREPARE STUFFING: Heat butter in a small pan, add mushrooms and spring onion and cook about 3 minutes or until soft. Remove from heat, add breadcrumbs and stir until combined.

4 Lay fillets, skin side up, and divide stuffing between fillets. Fold in half, with tail and head ends together and secure with satay skewers.

5 Lightly grease an ovenproof baking dish, place in fish, pour over wine and cover with a lid or foil. Bake in oven for about 6 minutes or until fillets have firmed a little. Remove and put on a plate. Strain cooking liquid and pour into stock.

6 Heat butter over a low heat. Add flour and cook for 3 to 4 minutes, stirring constantly. Off the heat gradually add stock, stirring constantly. Bring to the boil, reduce heat and simmer for 5 minutes, stirring occasionally. Taste and adjust seasoning, adding nutmeg to taste.

7 Combine egg yolk and sour cream. Add a spoonful of hot sauce and combine. Stir mixture into sauce and cook over a very gentle heat until thick. Do not boil. Cover surface of sauce with a piece of dampened greaseproof paper. Set aside to cool.

8 Grease work surface with half the oil. Coat both sides of fillets with cooled sauce. Remove satay skewers, place on oiled surface and leave until cold. Beat egg with remaining oil and put on a flat plate. Place breadcrumbs on a sheet of greaseproof paper. Dip fillets in egg and breadcrumbs.

9 Heat oil for deep-frying 190°C (375°F). Cook fillets in oil until golden. Drain on crumpled kitchen paper.

10 Serve hot, garnished with parsley and accompanied by hot tomato sauce.

SERVES 4

LEMON FLOUNDER

2 x 375 g flounder or plaice

plain flour

3 tablespoons butter

juice ½ large lemon

2 teaspoons chopped fresh parsley

salt and pepper

extra parsley, to garnish

1 Roll fish in flour, shaking off excess. Heat 1 tablespoon butter in pan. Fry fish until cooked on both sides, turning once. Place on serving dish and keep hot.

2 Clean and dry pan. Heat remaining butter, add lemon juice, parsley and seasonings. Cook until foaming, pour over fish and sprinkle with extra parsley. Serve with thin lemon slices.

SERVES 2

FILLETS *of* SOLE *with* WHITE WINE

6 spring onions, finely chopped

1 tablespoon chopped fresh parsley

100 g mushrooms, sliced

4 x 100 g fillets sole or flounder

salt and white pepper

⅔ cup (150 ml) dry white wine

1 cup (250 ml) Fish Stock (see recipe page 88)

90 g butter

juice ½ lemon

pinch cayenne pepper

500 g potatoes, peeled and steamed

1 Preheat oven to 200°C (400°F).

2 Sprinkle spring onions, parsley and mushrooms over base of a lightly greased, shallow baking dish.

3 Season fish fillets lightly with salt and pepper and arrange on vegetables. Combine wine and stock and pour over fish. Bring to the boil on top of the stove then cover and bake in oven for about 8 minutes or until the fish flakes when tested.

4 Carefully remove fish fillets to a flame-proof serving dish. Strain cooking liquid into a pan and place vegetables around fillets. Keep warm. Simmer cooking liquid until reduced by a third.

5 Cut the butter into pieces. Whisk butter into sauce, a piece at a time, until sauce is smooth and creamy. Taste and adjust seasoning with lemon juice.

6 Pour sauce over fish and sprinkle with cayenne pepper. Place under a preheated grill to brown sauce. Serve hot garnished with sliced potatoes.

SERVES 4

Fried Stuffed Fillets of Sole

PLAITED FILLETS
with FRIED PARSLEY

FRIED PARSLEY
oil for deep-frying
sprigs of fresh parsley

FISH
6 x 250 g fresh fillets (sole or flounder)
½ cup (60 g) seasoned plain flour
3 eggs, beaten
1½ cups (90 g) white breadcrumbs
oil for deep-frying
6 lemon wedges, pips removed
Tartare Sauce (see recipe page 89)

*Plaited Fillets
with Fried Parsley*

1 TO PREPARE FRIED PARSLEY: Preheat oil for deep-frying. Make sure the parsley is dry before you deep-fry it. Trim off excess stalks.

Drop the parsley, three sprigs at a time, into hot oil. When the spattering subsides, remove parsley quickly, so that it does not brown, and drain well on absorbent paper. The sprigs of fried parsley should be crisp and deep green. Set aside.

2 Remove any black and white skin from fillets and cut each lengthways into three pieces, leaving 1 cm uncut at one end of each fillet. Plait each fillet and secure the end with a toothpick.

3 Lightly toss fillets in seasoned flour, dip in beaten egg and coat with breadcrumbs. Deep-fry fillets at 185°C (360°F).

4 Serve garnished with fried parsley and lemon wedges and Tartare Sauce.

SERVES 6

POACHED SOLE *with* SEAFOOD

6 lemon sole or flounders, skinned and filleted

salt and pepper

90 g butter

24 mussels, cleaned

12 spring onions, sliced

1⅔ cups (400 ml) dry white wine

6 bottled oysters

1 onion, chopped

1 carrot, sliced

6 green king prawns (shrimps)

12 button mushrooms

juice 1 lemon

2 cups (500 ml) Fish Stock (see recipe page 88)

3 tablespoons plain flour

3 egg yolks

½ cup (125 ml) cream

croûtes, to garnish

1 Preheat oven to 180°C (350°F).

2 Check fillets for bones. Season lightly with salt and pepper.

3 In a pan place 15 g butter, mussels, pinch pepper, one-third of the spring onions and ½ cup (125 ml) wine. Cover, bring to the boil then simmer until shells open. Strain cooking liquid through 2 layers of damp muslin and reserve. Discard any mussels which remain closed.

4 Remove mussels from shells, place in a bowl and pour over strained cooking liquid from shells. Keep warm.

5 Place oysters in a small pan, cover with a little of the oyster liquor and simmer for 2 minutes. Strain and keep oysters warm; reserve liquid.

6 Place onion and carrot in a pan with ¾ cup (200 ml) wine, 2 cups (500 ml) water and salt and pepper to taste. Bring to the boil, reduce heat and add prawns. Simmer

until prawns change colour. Remove from heat and cool prawns in the liquid. Shell and devein.

7 Level stalk of mushrooms with cap, flute edges and reserve trimmings.

8 Place lemon juice, 2 teaspoons butter and ½ cup (125 ml) water in a pan. Bring to the boil, add mushrooms and simmer for 2 minutes. Drain, reserving liquid and keep mushrooms warm.

9 Grease a flameproof dish and place remaining spring onions and mushroom trimmings on the base. Place fish over vegetables and add stock, reserved cooking juices and remaining wine. Bring to the boil on top of stove, then cover and bake in oven for 15 minutes or until fish flakes easily when tested. Remove fish to a serving dish, keep warm and strain cooking liquid.

10 Heat 3 tablespoons butter and add flour. Cook for 3 minutes, stirring. Off the heat, gradually add reserved cooking liquid. Bring to the boil, reduce heat and simmer for 10 minutes, stirring occasionally.

11 Beat egg yolks and cream together. Add a little hot sauce to yolks and combine. Pour back into sauce and cook, stirring, over a very gentle heat until thickened. Do not boil. Remove from heat and stir through remaining butter.

12 Pour some of the sauce over fish and serve the rest in a sauce boat. Garnish fish with mussels, oysters, prawns, mushrooms, and croûtes. Serve hot.

SERVES 6

CROÛTES

Arrange 12 to 16 slices of French bread (about 2 cm thick) on a baking tray and bake in a preheated oven at 180°C (350°F) for 30 minutes or until bread is dried out and golden brown. Halfway through baking, baste bread with olive oil. After baking, rub bread with a clove of garlic cut in half.

POACHED SOLE WITH SEAFOOD

This is a dish for a very special occasion and for diners who will appreciate the effort involved. The traditional garnish includes crayfish but prawns can be used. If liked, substitute cooked crayfish tails.

CRÈME FRAÎCHE

Stir ¾ cup (180 ml) cream and 1 tablespoon plain yoghurt together in a jar and keep covered overnight or for 8 hours in a warm place. Alternatively, place loosely covered jar in microwave oven and cook on lowest temperature (50°C, 95°F) for 4 minutes. Before using chill well. It will thicken as it chills.

FILLETS *of* SOLE *with* MUSSELS *and* PRAWNS

1 cup (250 ml) dry white wine

60 g spring onions, finely chopped

2 bay leaves

1 kg mussels, scrubbed and beards removed

350 g large uncooked prawns (shrimps)

100 g butter

1.25 kg sole fillets (or flounder)

2½ cups (625 ml) Fish Stock (see recipe page 88)

1 tablespoon plain flour

1 cup (250 ml) Crème Fraîche or cream

3 egg yolks

white pepper

1 truffle, sliced (optional)

1 Preheat oven to 180°C (350°F).

2 Place wine, spring onions and bay leaves in a saucepan and bring to the boil. Simmer for 3 minutes.

3 Add mussels, cover and simmer for 5 minutes, shaking pan occasionally. Discard any mussels which remain closed. Strain ⅔ cup (150 ml) cooking liquid through two layers of damp muslin. Remove mussels from shells, reserving a few with shells intact for garnish.

4 Shell and devein prawns, leaving tails intact. Heat 30 g butter. Sauté prawns for 2 minutes, add mussels and keep warm.

5 Place sole fillets in a buttered, shallow baking dish. Pour the reserved, strained mussel liquid and stock over fish. Cover with foil and place in oven for 10 minutes or until the fish flakes easily when tested. Remove fish and keep warm, then boil cooking liquid until reduced by half. Allow to cool slightly.

6 Heat 30 g butter. Add flour and cook 1 minute, stirring over a moderate heat. Off the heat, gradually blend in the reduced liquid. Bring to the boil and simmer 3 minutes, stirring continuously.

7 Whisk together Crème Fraîche and egg yolks. Gradually add half the hot sauce. Whisk this mixture into remaining sauce and whisk continuously over a very gentle heat until thickened. Do not boil. Soften the remaining butter and gradually whisk into the sauce, off the heat. Stir in mussels and prawns.

8 Pour sauce over fish and garnish with reserved mussels and sliced truffles.

SERVES 6

FILLETS *of* SOLE *with* BASIL

350 g zucchini (courgettes), sliced

1 tablespoon oil

1 sprig rosemary

12 leaves fresh basil

salt and freshly ground black pepper

150 g tomatoes, peeled and chopped

a little plain flour

8 fillets of sole (or other white-fleshed fish)

80 g butter

breadcrumbs

extra basil leaves

1 lemon, sliced or cut in wedges

1 Preheat oven to 225°C (430°F).

2 In a pan, sauté zucchini in a little oil with rosemary, basil, salt and pepper. When nearly done, add tomatoes and sauté for a further 2 minutes.

3 Flour sole fillets and brown in butter.

4 Butter an ovenproof dish and arrange fillets in one row if possible. Cover with zucchini-tomato mixture, sprinkle with breadcrumbs, dot with butter and bake in the oven for 5 to 10 minutes until brown. Serve garnished with basil leaves and lemon wedges or slices.

SERVES 4

FLOUNDER MINERVA

4 x 150 g flounder fillets

2 tablespoons butter

60 g mushrooms, sliced

125 g seedless green grapes

**1¼ cups (300 ml) Fish Stock
(see recipe page 88)**

2 tablespoons plain flour

1 egg yolk

⅔ cup (150 ml) cream

juice ½ lemon

salt

pinch cayenne pepper

750 g potatoes, cooked and mashed

1 egg, beaten

**125 g cooked crayfish meat, cut into
1.5 cm pieces**

1 Preheat oven to 200°C (400°F).

2 Wipe fish fillets and check for bones.

3 Grease an ovenproof dish with
1 tablespoon butter. Place fillets, mushrooms
and grapes in dish. Cover with stock. Cover
dish with a sheet of buttered greaseproof
paper and bake in preheated oven for
20 minutes. Strain cooking liquid and
reserve. Keep fish mixture warm.

4 Heat remaining butter in a pan, add flour
and cook for 2 to 3 minutes. Gradually add
reserved stock off the heat, stirring
constantly. Bring to the boil, reduce heat
and simmer for 3 minutes.

5 Blend egg yolk and cream. Pour ½ cup
(125 ml) hot sauce onto cream and whisk
well. Pour back into pan and heat through
over a low heat. Do not allow sauce to
boil. Stir in lemon juiceand season to taste
with salt and cayenne pepper.

6 Blend potato with a little butter and
milk. Put potato into a piping bag fitted
with a fluted nozzle and pipe potato around
the edge of a shallow flameproof dish; brush
with beaten egg.

7 Arrange fish, mushrooms, grapes and
crayfish meat in dish and cover with sauce.
Place dish under a preheated hot grill for
5 minutes or until potato is browned and
sauce glazed. Serve hot with spinach.

SERVES 4

SKATE *with* BLACK BUTTER

185 g unsalted butter

1 kg skate wings

**2½ cups (600 ml) Fish Stock
(See recipe page 88)**

⅓ cup (80 ml) vinegar

extra 2 tablespoons vinegar

1 tablespoon chopped fresh parsley

2 tablespoons capers

1 Heat butter in a pan until hot. Remove
from the heat and allow to stand until milk
solids settle to base of pan. Carefully pour
clarified butter into another container,
leaving milk solids behind.

2 Wipe the skate wings and cut into equal
serving-size pieces. Plunge skate into
boiling water for 4 minutes. Cool slightly.
Remove skin.

3 Place stock and vinegar in pan and bring
to the boil. Add skate and poach for
12 minutes or until tender. Drain well
and pat dry. Place on a serving dish and
keep warm.

4 Heat clarified butter in pan until it is
brown and foaming but not black. Sprinkle
vinegar over skate then pour over the butter.
Sprinkle with parsley and capers. Serve hot
with buttered boiled potatoes.

SERVES 4

**SKATE WITH
BLACK BUTTER**

*This is a classic French
recipe. Only the 'wings'
of skate are ever used
as food.*

CRUSTACEANS

Prawns, crab, crayfish, lobster — much loved and healthy too.
It is most important to buy the freshest possible crustaceans. Prawns
should be firm and have a pleasant smell. If buying dead crabs, they should
have limbs intact and feel heavy not hollow when picked up, however crabs
other than blue swimmer crabs should be alive until point of cooking as
they go bad very quickly. Crayfish and lobster can be bought alive or
cooked. If cooked, they should be intact and have a pleasant sea smell.

Live crabs and lobsters should never be put into boiling water — drown or
freeze them first, then put in cold water and bring to the boil.

Cooking with seafood is fun and easy. Cook prawns in soup, batter, in prawn
balls or puffs, and with all sorts of sauces. Of course we have included such
favourites as garlic prawns. Learn how to prepare a crab and cook it in style,
and try lobster with pernod sauce or tomato and wine. You can't go past the
famous paella, a rice dish with a mixture of seafood, chicken and vegetables.

Remember you don't need to spend lots of money on huge quantities of
seafood as only a small amount is necessary to make a meal very special.

The batter for tempura should be light, crisp and thin, so that the food shows through the cooked batter. Tempura is served with a dipping sauce garnished with white radish and green ginger.

SEAFOOD COCKTAIL

200 g each prepared crab, lobster, prawns (shrimps)

¼ lettuce, finely shredded

½ cup (125 ml) Cocktail Sauce (see recipe page 91)

4 teaspoons red or black caviar

4 lemon wedges, pips removed

4 parsley sprigs

triangles of buttered bread

1 TO PREPARE SEAFOOD: Shred the white meat of the crab; chop lobster into 1.5 cm dice; peel, remove intestinal track and wash prawns. Cut large prawns into two to three pieces.

2 Place a small amount of lettuce in each cocktail glass. Add the prepared shellfish, coat with Cocktail Sauce and top each with 1 teaspoon of caviar.

3 To decorate, cut into the white of the lemon wedge and set this on the edge of the glass. Place a sprig of parsley beside the lemon wedge inside the glass and serve with triangles of buttered bread.

SERVES 4

DASHI

Rinse a 5 cm square of kelp seaweed and wipe lightly with kitchen paper. Place in a pan with 2½ cups (600 ml) water and bring to the boil. Remove seaweed and add 10 g dried bonito fish. Remove from the heat and stand, covered, for 2 minutes. Strain and add 1 teaspoon Japanese soy sauce. Note: If preferred, fish stock can be used instead of dashi, but the flavour will be slightly different.

SEAFOOD *in* BATTER

500 g prawns (shrimps), shelled and deveined

250 g snapper fillets, skinned, boned and cut in strips

125 g snow peas

oil for deep frying

BATTER

½ cup (60 g) plain flour

½ cup (60 g) cornflour

1½ teaspoons baking powder

salt

1 egg

¾ cup (180 ml) iced water

DIPPING SAUCE

1¾ cup (450 ml) Dashi (see recipe below)

1 to 2 tablespoons Japanese soy sauce

2 tablespoons rice wine or dry sherry

GARNISH

2 tablespoons grated green ginger

4 teaspoons finely grated white radish

1 TO MAKE BATTER: Sift flours, baking powder and salt to taste into a chilled bowl. Beat the egg and water together. Pour into flour mixture and stir gently to combine. Do not overmix. Add one ice cube to mixture to help keep cold.

2 Heat oil for deep frying to 180°C (350°F). Combine ingredients for the dipping sauce, stir well and heat through while frying tempura.

3 Dip prawns, fish and snow peas into batter one piece at a time and drain off excess batter. Cook a few pieces at a time in oil until light golden in colour. Drain well on crumpled kitchen paper and arrange decoratively.

4 Serve hot dipping sauce in individual bowls, with 1 teaspoon grated radish and ½ teaspoon ginger in each bowl.

SERVES 4

CROSTINI *with* HOT SEAFOOD

50 g butter

250 g (net weight) seafood: prawns (shrimps), scallops, oysters, etc, finely chopped

1 clove garlic, crushed

1 teaspoon tomato paste

1 tablespoon chopped fresh parsley or basil

3 tablespoons white wine

salt and pepper

oil

8 slices French bread

1 Melt butter in a small pan and add seafood, garlic, tomato paste and parsley or basil. Moisten with white wine and simmer for 2 minutes.

2 Add freshly ground pepper and a little salt if necessary.

3 Fry bread in a little oil and top it with mixture. Serve immediately.

SERVES 4

Seafood in Batter

CROSTINI

Crostini are a typical feature of Italian snack bars. The variety of their toppings is endless. At home they are often served between meals or as a light first course.

LEBANESE CUCUMBERS

These are also called European cucumbers. They are smaller than common cucumbers and have a softer skin.

STUFFED CUCUMBER

1 Lebanese cucumber

1 small bunch watercress

90 g crabmeat, canned or fresh

¼ teaspoon grated fresh ginger

3 teaspoons soy or tamari sauce

1 Cut a lengthways slit down cucumber only as deep as the seeds. Try to avoid halving cucumber. Using the handle of a teaspoon, scrape out and discard seeds.

2 Blanch watercress sprigs in boiling water for 30 seconds only. Drain and cool immediately with water.

3 Pick over crabmeat, discarding any cartilage. Drain well, squeezing all liquid from crab. Combine crab and ginger.

4 Holding cucumber slightly open, spoon in crab mixture and top with watercress

Stuffed Cucumber

Scrape out and discard seeds.

Spoon in crab mixture.

leaves, reserving some for garnishing. Press together gently. Wrap securely in plastic wrap and refrigerate for 30 minutes.

5 Cut cucumber in 2 cm slices and arrange on a serving plate. Sprinkle with soy or tamari sauce. Garnish with remaining watercress sprigs.

SERVES 4 TO 6

PRAWNS PROVENÇALE

500 g uncooked prawns (shrimps)

seasoned plain flour

2½ tablespoons cooking oil

1 small clove garlic, chopped

250 g ripe tomatoes, peeled, seeded and chopped

2 tablespoons dry white wine

½ cup (125 ml) Fresh Tomato Sauce (see recipe page 91)

coarsely chopped fresh parsley

lime or lemon slices and parsley sprigs, to garnish

1 Lightly coat prawns with seasoned flour and shake off the surplus.

2 Heat 2 tablespoons of oil in a frying pan and add prawns, frying to a light golden brown colour and tossing frequently. Drain prawns well.

3 Fry garlic in remaining oil in a saucepan for a few seconds, pour off any surplus oil then add tomatoes, cooking them for 8 to 10 minutes.

4 Add white wine and Fresh Tomato Sauce and bring to the boil. Adjust seasonings to taste and stir in chopped parsley. Now gently fold prawns through sauce. Serve on individual plates, garnished with lime or lemon slices and sprigs of parsley.

SERVES 4

SEAFOOD VOL-AU-VENT

Add lobster to this as well, if desired. Halve a lobster, remove and slice flesh and add it to the seafood mixture.

4 vol-au-vent cases, precooked

30 g butter

1 tablespoon fresh lemon juice

60 g button mushrooms, diced

250 g cooked prawns (shrimps), peeled and deveined

125 g mussel meat

125 g scallop meat

½ cup (125 ml) White Wine Sauce (see recipe page 90)

chopped fresh parsley

salt and pepper

1 Warm vol-au-vent cases while preparing the seafood mixture.

2 Poach mussel and scallop meat in simmering water for a few minutes. Drain and cool.

3 In a pan heat butter and lemon juice and sauté mushrooms for 2 to 3 minutes. Add prepared seafood, White Wine Sauce, parsley and seasonings.

4 Spoon seafood mixture into warm vol-au-vent cases and serve on individual plates.

SERVES 4

 BUTTON MUSHROOMS

Store unwashed in a brown paper bag in the refrigerator for up to 7 days. Wipe clean just before using. Don't peel them as the skin has the most nutrients.

Seafood Vol-au-Vent

 SEAFOOD VOL-AU-VENT

Mussel and scallop meat can be poached with some fresh herbs and lemon rind, for extra flavour.

Prawns *in* Almond Sauce

4 cups (1 litre) water

1 stalk celery, roughly sliced

½ teaspoon black peppercorns

3 allspice berries

1 kg green prawns (shrimps), washed, shelled
and deveined

5 slices stale white bread, crusts removed

1½ cups (375 ml) milk

90 g butter

2 onions, finely chopped

2 cloves garlic, crushed

1 teaspoon paprika

¼ to ½ teaspoon chilli powder

125 g ground almonds

freshly ground black pepper

fresh parsley, to garnish

1 Place water, celery, peppercorns and allspice berries in a saucepan. Bring to the boil, add prawns and simmer, covered, for 4 minutes or until cooked. Drain prawns and reserve 1½ cups (375 ml) of liquid.

2 Dry prawns on absorbent paper. Soak bread in milk for 5 minutes. Drain, reserving milk, and mash bread until nearly smooth.

3 Heat butter in a frying pan. Add onions and garlic and cook over medium heat for about 8 minutes.

4 Add paprika and chilli powder and cook, stirring, for 30 seconds. Add bread and cook for 5 minutes, stirring frequently. Add almonds, reserved milk and prawn liquid and bring to the boil, stirring until thickened. Reduce heat, add prawns and heat through. Season with pepper to taste. Serve hot, garnished with parsley.

SERVES 4 TO 6

Prawn Puffs

Royal red prawnmeat is suitable for this dish, otherwise choose school prawns (shrimps). If ocean perch fillets are not available choose any other favourite fillet.

180 g cooked peeled prawnmeat

180 g ocean perch fillets, cooked and flaked

2 teaspoons butter

2 teaspoons plain flour

½ cup (125 ml) milk

1 teaspoon chopped fresh parsley

½ teaspoon chopped fennel (optional)

fresh lemon juice

few drops Tabasco sauce

salt

paprika

500 g frozen puff pastry, thawed

oil for deep frying

1 If prawns are large, cut into smaller pieces and combine with fish. Set aside.

2 In a small pan, heat butter. Add flour and cook for 1 minute. Remove from heat and add milk, stirring constantly. Return to heat and cook, stirring, until sauce simmers and thickens. Remove from heat and cover surface of sauce with a piece of dampened greaseproof paper; set aside to cool.

3 Remove paper from sauce. Add prawns, fish, parsley, fennel, lemon juice to taste and Tabasco sauce. Season with salt and paprika to taste.

4 Roll out pastry on a lightly floured board until 6 mm thick. Cut pastry into circles, using a 12.5 cm round cutter.

5 Place a spoonful of filling in centre of pastry. Brush edges with water, fold over and seal well.

6 Heat oil to 190°C (375°F). Deep fry puffs in batches until golden brown, about 4 minutes. Drain well on crumpled kitchen paper. Serve hot.

SERVES 4 TO 6

GARLIC PRAWNS

750 g medium green prawns (shrimps)

⅓ cup (80 ml) olive oil

4 large cloves garlic, sliced

2 bay leaves

⅓ cup (80 ml) Aïoli (see Mayonnaise recipe page 89)

1 sprig fresh thyme or ¼ teaspoon dried thyme

1 tablespoon fresh lemon juice

freshly ground black pepper

1 Shell the prawns, leaving head and tail shell intact, then devein.

2 Heat oil in a heavy-based frying pan over a moderate heat. Add garlic and cook until it starts to colour. Drain and discard.

3 Increase heat and when oil is moderately hot, 190°C (375°F), add prawns and bay leaves, stirring constantly for about 5 minutes until prawns are cooked.

4 Remove pan from heat and carefully stir through aïoli, thyme and lemon juice. Divide between individual serving plates and grind black pepper over each plate before serving. Serve hot with crusty bread.

SERVES 4

PREPARING PRAWNS (SHRIMPS)

Cut off the head, remove the tail and shell. Use a sharp knife to devein them. Prawns can be cooked in many ways including grilling, frying, barbecuing and are done when they turn red.

Heat oil, add prawns and bay leaves.

Carefully stir through aïoli, thyme and lemon juice.

Garlic Prawns

Lemon Grass and Chilli Prawns

LEMON GRASS *and* CHILLI PRAWNS

These prawns are very spicy. To lessen the effect of the chilli, remove the seeds. Also, add only half the amount of masala suggested. The masala will keep for up to 2 weeks in the refrigerator if stored in a covered bowl.

1 kg green prawns (shrimps)

3 tablespoons oil, for frying

MASALA

1 onion, chopped

6 cloves garlic, chopped

½ teaspoon turmeric

1 cm piece cinnamon stick

1 cm piece ginger root, finely grated

20 fresh red chillies (split and seeds removed if preferred)

grated rind and juice 1 lime or lemon

5 cm piece lemon grass, cut into 1 cm pieces

1 TO PREPARE MASALA: Place onion in the container of a food processor with garlic, turmeric, cinnamon stick, ginger and chillies. Blend until finely chopped. Add lime rind and juice. Stir through the lemon grass pieces.

2 Peel prawns, leaving tail intact and remove veins. Place in a glass or ceramic bowl and add half of the masala. Store remaining masala in a covered small bowl for another day. Stir to evenly distribute the mixture through the prawns. Cover and marinate for 2 hours in the refrigerator.

3 Heat oil in a wok or frying pan and add prawns. Stir-fry over high heat for 5 minutes or until just cooked. Serve hot with rice.

SERVES 4

SATAY PRAWNS

1 kg green king prawns (shrimps), shelled, deveined and washed

½ cup (125 ml) Tomato Sauce (see recipe page 91)

SATAY MARINADE

3 cloves garlic, crushed

¼ teaspoon dried chillis

½ teaspoon dried chilli powder

pinch of salt

2 tablespoons fresh lemon juice

1 teaspoon finely grated lemon rind

2 tablespoons soy sauce

1 teaspoon honey

oil

1 Combine marinade ingredients. Mix well.

2 Allow prawns to marinate in satay for 30 minutes. Brush barbecue plate with oil and stir-fry prawns for 2 to 3 minutes or until cooked.

NOTE: If using open grill, thread prawns onto bamboo skewers.

SERVES 4 AS AN ENTRÉE

STEP-BY-STEP TECHNIQUES

DRESSED CRAB

1 x 1.5 kg green crab
1 tablespoon fresh breadcrumbs
2 tablespoons chopped fresh parsley
salt and pepper
cayenne pepper
juice 1 lemon
1 egg, hard-boiled
1 tablespoon capers

1 Scrub crab well and place in a large pan with water to cover. Slowly bring to the boil, reduce heat and simmer for 20 minutes. Turn off heat and allow crab to cool in the water.

2 Twist legs and claws from body. Twist off claw pincers. Crack open claws and large legs with a hammer or the handle of a heavy knife and remove white meat with a skewer.

3 Place crab on its back on a large chopping board, face end away, grasp hold of shell and push off the body with thumbs. Remove and discard greyish white stomach sac from behind head, known as 'dead men's fingers'. Scrape out soft brown meat and discard. Cut body part in half and remove any white meat from leg sockets.

4 Using handle of a heavy knife, tap away shell along the natural dark line around rim. Scrub shell under cold running water, dry and brush with oil.

5 Remove all white meat and place in a bowl. Add breadcrumbs and half the chopped parsley and season with salt, pepper, cayenne pepper and lemon juice.

6 Place white meat mixture in shell.

7 Finely chop egg white and push yolk through a sieve. Garnish crab with strips of yolk, white, remaining parsley and capers.

SERVES 4

Twist legs and claws from body.

Place crab on its back, push off body with thumbs.

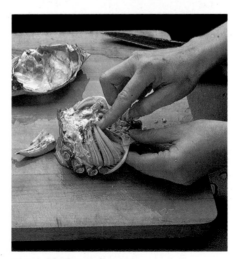

Remove 'dead men's fingers'.

 **DRESSED CRAB**

Serve this colourful and impressive dish cold with a green salad and crusty bread and butter.

Baked Crayfish

MARYLAND STEAMED CRABS

1 kg blue swimmer crabs, uncooked

2 cups (500 ml) vinegar

2 cups (500 ml) water

3 teaspoons dry mustard

1 teaspoon chilli powder, or to taste

1 Wipe the crabs over.

2 Place vinegar and water in a steamer.

3 Place crabs on a rack and season with mustard and chilli. Place rack in steamer, cover tightly and bring to the boil. Reduce heat and simmer for 10 to 15 minutes or until crabs are cooked. Serve with crusty bread and butter and tossed salad.

SERVES 4

BAKED CRAYFISH

This is an easy dish for a special occasion that does not require much time in the kitchen.

BAKED CRAYFISH

2 large green crayfish tails

1 small clove garlic, crushed

½ cup (125 ml) oil

3 tablespoons brandy

juice 1 lemon

salt and cayenne pepper

lemon wedges

1 Preheat oven to 200°C (400°F).

2 Split crayfish tails lengthways. Combine garlic, oil, brandy and lemon juice.

3 Season crayfish with salt and cayenne pepper and brush with the oil mixture.

4 Place crayfish in a baking tray and bake for 15 to 20 minutes or until heated through. Baste several times during cooking. Serve with lemon wedges.

SERVES 4

CRAYFISH *with* PERNOD SAUCE

2 x 1.5 kg crayfish, cooked

2 tablespoons oil

1 small onion, finely chopped

100 g mushrooms, diced

2 stalks celery, diced

1½ cups (90 g) fresh white breadcrumbs

¾ cup (180 ml) dry white wine

3 tablespoons butter

3 tablespoons plain flour

1¼ cup (300 ml) milk

salt and white pepper

1 egg, hard-boiled and chopped

½ teaspoon prepared mustard

3 tablespoons Pernod

juice 1 large lemon

1 cup grated cheese

1 tablespoon chopped parsley

Halve the tail lengthwise.

Add sauce to breadcrumb mixture.

Divide mixture between the shells.

1 Cut head from tail of crayfish. Halve tail lengthways, remove meat and clean shells.

2 Heat oil, add prepared vegetables and cook until soft. Add breadcrumbs and wine and bring to the boil. Remove from the heat.

3 Melt butter, add flour and cook for 2 minutes, stirring. Take off heat, gradually add milk, stirring. Return to heat, bring to the boil and simmer for 3 minutes. Season with salt and pepper.

4 Add this white sauce to the vegetable mixture, stir well to combine and bring to the boil.

5 Stir through the egg, mustard and Pernod. Cook over a gentle heat for 5 minutes. Add crayfish meat and heat through. Divide mixture between shells.

6 Sprinkle with lemon juice and cheese. Cook under a preheated grill until cheese melts and turns golden. Sprinkle with chopped parsley.

SERVES 4

LOBSTER WITH TOMATO AND WINE

If lobster is unavailable, crayfish is a suitable substitute for this dish.

CLEANING CRABS

Scrub crab well and place in pan with water to cover. Bring to the boil, simmer 20 minutes. Allow crab to cool in water. Twist legs, claws and pincers from body. Crack open claws and remove white meat. Place crab on its back and push body off shell. Discard stomach sac ('dead men's fingers'). Discard any soft brown meat.

PASTA BASKET *with* MARINARA SAUCE

250 g egg noodles

3 cups oil for deep-frying

MARINARA SAUCE

500 g green prawns (shrimps), shelled and veins removed

3 calamari (squid), cleaned and sliced

250 g scallops

½ cup (125 ml) dry white wine

½ cup (125 ml) water

2 tablespoons oil

5 large tomatoes, peeled and chopped

2 cloves garlic, crushed

1 tablespoon tomato paste

8 oysters

45 g canned anchovies, drained

salt

freshly ground black pepper

1 tablespoon chopped fresh parsley

Parmesan cheese, to serve

1 TO PREPARE BASKETS: Cook egg noodles in boiling salted water for 8 minutes, then drain. Using a metal strainer, place a quarter of the noodles into the strainer to form a 'basket' shape. Place a second strainer over the top of the noodles to hold them in place.

2 Heat the oil and, when it's very hot, lower the strainer into it. Cook noodles until crisp and golden brown, then remove noodle basket from the strainers and allow to drain. Repeat with remaining noodles to make three more baskets.

3 TO PREPARE SAUCE: Simmer prawns, calamari, scallops, wine and water in a large saucepan for 1 minute, then remove the seafood and set aside.

4 Heat oil in frying pan, stir in tomatoes, garlic and tomato paste and cook for 2 minutes. Add cooked seafood plus oysters and anchovies to the pan and heat through. Season with salt and pepper and add parsley.

5 Place noodle baskets on serving plates and spoon over the Marinara Sauce. Serve hot with a sprinkling of Parmesan cheese.

SERVES 4

LOBSTER *with* TOMATO *and* WINE

1 x 2 kg freshly killed crayfish

salt and cayenne pepper

30 g butter

1 tablespoon oil

1 onion, finely chopped

4 spring onions, sliced

3 tablespoons brandy

3 tablespoons white wine

3 tablespoons Fish Stock (see recipe page 88)

3 tomatoes, peeled, seeded and chopped

1 teaspoon tomato paste or granules

extra 30 g butter

fresh herbs, to garnish

1 Split crayfish in half lengthways, cut off head section and reserve roe. Twist off claws and cut tail section into pieces. Season tail pieces with salt and cayenne pepper.

2 Heat butter and oil in frying pan. Add crayfish pieces, legs and onion and cook over a gentle heat for 4 minutes.

3 Add spring onions and cook for a further minute. Pour in heated brandy and flame. Shake pan until flames die down. Stir in remaining ingredients except extra butter and herbs. Bring to the boil, reduce heat and simmer for 15 minutes, stirring occasionally.

4 Remove crayfish and keep warm on a serving dish.

5 Simmer sauce to thicken it slightly then stir through roe and butter. Push through a sieve or purée in a blender. Taste and adjust seasonings and reheat. Coat crayfish with sauce and serve garnished with herbs.

SERVES 4 (AS AN ENTRÉE)

TOULON CRAB

5 blue swimmer crabs, cooked

250 g mussels, scrubbed and cleaned

2 eggs, hard-boiled and chopped

1 clove garlic, crushed

2 teaspoons fresh fennel, chopped

juice ½ lemon

pinch cayenne pepper

salt and pepper

½ cup (125 ml) cream

1 cup grated cheese

1 Clean crabs, but do not prepare shells. Reserve shells and place the meat in a pan.

2 Place mussels in a separate pan with a little water and simmer, covered, until they open. Twist off top shell, tip shell liquid onto crabmeat and remove mussels from shells. Add to crabmeat with eggs, garlic, fennel, lemon juice, cayenne, salt and pepper and cream. Heat over a low heat and divide between the four shells.

3 Sprinkle cheese over filled crabs and cook under a preheated grill until cheese melts. Serve hot with potatoes and a green salad.

SERVES 4

Pasta Basket with Marinara Sauce

PAELLA

Chorizo is a Spanish sausage. If unavailable substitute a peppery salami.

Paella

PAELLA

250 g calamari (squid)

4 to 6 chicken thighs

salt and pepper

½ teaspoon paprika

3 tablespoons oil

1½ cups (375 ml) water

1 cup (250 ml) dry white wine

1 bay leaf

125 g chorizo, sliced diagonally

4 baby octopus, cleaned and halved

2 green capsicum (peppers), sliced

4 tomatoes, peeled, seeded and chopped

1 onion, finely chopped

pinch saffron threads

¾ cup (150 g) long grain rice

300 g mussels, scrubbed and cleaned

500 g medium or large green prawns (shrimps)

1 Pull out and discard intestines of the calamari. Cut off tentacles and set aside. Discard 'feather' from calamari, then rinse and rub off skin. Rinse again.

2 Season chicken thighs with salt, pepper and paprika. Heat oil in a heavy-based frying pan or paellera. Cook chicken in oil until golden on both sides. Reduce heat.

3 Carefully cover with water, white wine and bay leaf and simmer for 15 minutes. Drain chicken and strain 2 cups (500 ml) of cooking liquid.

4 Add chorizo to pan and cook for 4 minutes, turning. Add prepared calamari,

octopus, capsicum, tomatoes, onion and saffron. Cover and cook over a gentle heat for 10 minutes, stirring occasionally.

5 Sprinkle rice over vegetables and pour over 1½ cups (375 ml) strained cooking liquid. Bring to the boil, reduce heat and simmer, covered, for 20 minutes, stirring occasionally.

6 Place mussels, prawns and chicken thighs over rice. Test rice and add more stock if necessary. Cover and cook over a gentle heat until rice is tender and mussels and prawns cooked. Serve from the dish.

SERVES 4 TO 6

RICE SALAD

1 kg mussels

½ cup (125 ml) dry white wine

1 cup (200 g) rice

2 lemons

6 tablespoons olive oil

salt and pepper

1 small bunch parsley, finely chopped

3 anchovy fillets, chopped

500 g freshly cooked king prawns (shrimps), shelled

1 Brush mussels under running water to free the shells of grit. Discard any open ones. Put them in a wide pan with the wine and bring to the boil. Lift them out as soon as they open. Shell approximately half of them, reserving the other half for decoration.

2 Boil rice in salted water, drain and run some cold water through it to separate the grains. Season it with juice of half a lemon, oil, plenty of pepper, parsley and anchovy fillets. Add salt if necessary.

3 Just before serving, stir the prawns into the rice, reserving some for decoration. Arrange the rice in a glass bowl and decorate it with reserved prawns, mussels in shells and lemon slices. Serve very cold.

SERVES 4

RISOTTO *with* PRAWNS

80 g butter

1 tablespoon oil

1 small onion, finely chopped

1 small carrot, finely chopped

1 small celery stalk, finely chopped

1 pinch thyme

½ cup (125 ml) white wine

500 g peeled green prawns (shrimps), halved if large

½ cup (125 ml) brandy

4 cups (1 litre) Fish Stock (see recipe page 88)

2½ cups (500 g) rice

1 Melt butter and oil in a heavy pan and sauté onion, carrot and celery until translucent.

2 Add thyme and wine and let it simmer until reduced by half.

3 Add prawns and simmer until they change colour — no longer or they will become tough. Take the pan off the stove and flambé with the brandy. Put it aside.

4 Separately, bring the stock to the boil and pour in the rice. Cook it until 'al dente'. Drain if necessary and stir through a tablespoon of butter.

5 Now delicately mix through the prawns and their juice and serve immediately.

SERVES 4

 MUSSELS

Only buy mussels which have closed shells. If open, the mussels are dead. Don't store live mussels in the refrigerator. Cook mussels quickly as they toughen easily.

MOLLUSCS

Molluscs (or shellfish) include mussels, oysters, scallops, calamari (squid), cuttlefish and octopus. They are low in cholesterol and similar to other seafood in many beneficial nutrients.

When buying molluscs, fresh is best: mussels should have shells tightly closed; oysters should be alive if bought in the shell; scallops can be bought shelled or unshelled; calamari rings should be white; cuttlefish and octopus should have firm flesh but don't worry if the ink sac is broken. For all of these, a pleasant sea smell is a good indication of freshness.

Preparation of the various shellfish is explained in the recipes in easy-to-follow instructions.

Mussels are ideal for entreés and sauces and as garnish for other dishes. They look terrific in a salad. Try peppered calamari or barbecued octopus for an unforgettable barbecue.

Grilling, baking, barbecuing, frying, all methods of cooking can be used with shellfish, and you can be creative with whatever sauce, herbs and flavouring take your fancy.

Fish Soup *with* Pepper Sauce

4 cups (1 litre) Fish Stock (see recipe page 88)

½ cup (125 ml) white wine

250 g tomatoes, peeled, seeded and sliced

1 clove garlic, chopped

2 strips orange rind

2 sprigs fresh parsley and fennel

sprig fresh thyme

pinch saffron threads

ROUILLE

1 green capsicum (pepper), halved

1 fresh chilli, halved and seeded

2 to 3 cloves garlic

250 g can red pimento

1½ tablespoons olive oil

fresh white breadcrumbs

FISH

750 g fish fillets (mixture of snapper, jewfish, whiting), cut in 3 cm wide strips

250 g green prawns (shrimps), shelled and deveined

375 g mussels, cleaned

4 green king prawns (shrimps), for garnish

1 Place stock, wine, tomatoes, garlic, orange rind, herbs and saffron in a saucepan. Bring to the boil, reduce heat and simmer for 20 minutes, then strain. Set aside.

2 TO PREPARE ROUILLE: Place capsicum and chilli in a pan, cover with cold water,

Fish Soup with Pepper Sauce

bring to the boil and simmer for 3 minutes. Drain well and refresh under cold running water.

3 Using a mortar and pestle, crush garlic and pimento. Add blanched capsicum and chilli and when smooth gradually add oil. Add enough breadcrumbs to form a firm mixture. Taste and adjust seasoning.

4 Bring reserved cooking liquid to the boil. Add fish and simmer for 2 minutes. Add prawns and mussels and simmer until all seafood is cooked, about 5 minutes. Discard any mussels that remain closed.

5 Fry the prawns for garnish in a little oil until colour changes. Garnish soup with prawns. Serve the soup hot topped with a spoonful of rouille and with crusty bread.

SERVES 4

CALAMARI *and* PRAWN HOT SOUP

250 g calamari (squid)

4 cups (1 litre) chicken stock

1 stalk lemon grass or 2 strips lemon rind

50 g red king prawns (shrimps), deveined and halved

1 to 2 teaspoons Thai fish sauce

1 to 2 fresh chillies, seeded and sliced

2 cloves garlic, crushed

juice 1 lime

chopped fresh coriander, to garnish

1 Clean calamari, cut body hood into strips and chop tentacles.

2 Bring stock and lemon grass or rind to the boil, reduce heat and simmer for 5 minutes.

3 Add calamari, prawns and half the fish sauce to the saucepan. Immediately stir through chillies. Taste and adjust seasoning.

4 Combine garlic and lime juice, stir through soup and serve hot, garnished with coriander.

SERVES 4 TO 6

PEPPERED CALAMARI

For those that like something with a bite, great for barbecues!

500 g calamari (squid) hoods, cut into rings

1 tablespoon cracked pepper

1 tablespoon oil

MARINADE

1 cup (250 ml) port or red wine

½ cup (125 ml) olive oil

1 small onion, roughly sliced

4 cloves garlic, crushed

3 bay leaves

¼ teaspoon salt

1 TO PREPARE MARINADE: In a bowl combine marinade ingredients. Mix well.

2 Place calamari rings in the marinade and allow to stand overnight. Drain marinade and sprinkle black pepper over squid.

3 Brush barbecue plate with oil, cook calamari on hot plate for 30 seconds. Serve with crusty bread.

SERVES 4 TO 6

Calamari and Prawn Hot Soup

 THAI FISH SAUCE

Thai fish sauce can be bought from most delicatessens and Asian groceries.

MARINARA SALAD

500 g shell-shaped pasta

SALAD

2 tablespoons oil

1 bunch spring onions, thinly sliced

2 cloves garlic, finely chopped

2 cups (500 ml) Fish Stock (see recipe page 88)

500 g scallops

500 g uncooked peeled prawns (shrimps), heads removed

2 large carrots, julienned

4 cups (1 litre) water

juice 1 lemon

1 teaspoon salt

6 tablespoons chopped fresh dill

freshly ground black pepper

WARM DRESSING

2 cloves garlic, crushed

1 teaspoon salt

6 tablespoons chopped fresh parsley

1 bunch fresh dill, chopped

2 tablespoons grated Parmesan cheese

½ cup (125 ml) chicken stock

½ cup (125 ml) oil

juice 1 lemon and grated rind ½ lemon

1 Combine dressing ingredients, mix well and set aside in a small saucepan.

2 TO PREPARE SALAD: Heat oil and sauté spring onions and garlic until softened. Add fish stock. Reduce heat, add scallops and poach for 1 to 2 minutes only. Remove with slotted spoon and keep warm.

3 Add prawns to stock and remove as soon as they turn opaque. Add to reserved scallops. Do not overcook as both will shrink and lose their taste. Increase heat to reduce stock to approximately half quantity. Add all remaining ingredients.

4 To assemble, cook pasta until 'al dente', drain well. Heat dressing, pour over pasta and mix well. Serve pasta topped with seafood mixture at room temperature.

SERVES 8

SCALLOPS BRETON STYLE

500 g scallops

60 g butter

6 to 8 spring onions, chopped

¾ cup (180 ml) dry white wine

salt and white pepper

2 tablespoons plain flour

1 egg yolk

½ cup (125 ml) cream

1 Separate body and roe of scallops.

2 Heat 30 g butter and fry spring onions until soft. Add scallops, wine, salt and pepper and just cover with water. Bring to the boil. Cook over a very gentle heat until scallops are tender.

3 Drain scallops, reserving cooking liquid and divide scallops between four individual flameproof serving dishes. Keep warm.

4 Heat remaining butter, add flour and cook, stirring, for 2 minutes. Gradually pour in strained cooking liquid, stirring constantly. Bring to the boil, reduce heat and simmer for 5 minutes.

5 Beat egg yolk lightly with a fork and pour on 2 tablespoons hot sauce, whisking constantly. Return egg yolk mixture to saucepan and heat through over a gentle heat. Off the heat, add cream very carefully as it may curdle.

6 Pour sauce over scallops and place under a preheated grill to brown. Serve with rice and a green salad.

SERVES 4

Shred ginger.

Stir fry pork and abalone over high heat.

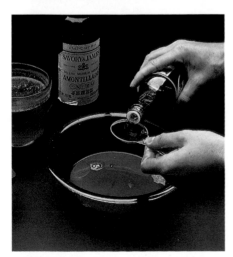

Combine liquids.

PORK *and* ABALONE SOUP

125 g lean pork

125 g canned abalone

2 tablespoons oil

4 cups (1 litre) chicken stock

2 tablespoons dry sherry

2 tablespoons soy sauce

1 teaspoon shredded green ginger

60 g bamboo shoot, diced

1 spring onion, to garnish

1 Thinly slice pork and cut into pieces about 2.5 cm square. Prepare abalone in the same way, reserving any liquid.

2 Heat oil, add pork and abalone, and cook over a high heat until meat changes colour. Drain.

3 Combine reserved abalone liquid, stock, sherry and soy sauce and bring to the boil. Add ginger and bamboo shoot, reduce heat and simmer for 2 minutes. Add pork and abalone, heat through and garnish.

SERVES 4

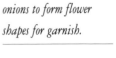

SERVING PORK AND ABALONE SOUP

Serve hot with chilli sauce and slice spring onions to form flower shapes for garnish.

Pork and Abalone Soup

SCALLOPS *and* MUSHROOMS *in* WINE SAUCE

500 g scallops
1¼ cups (300 ml) dry white wine
few peppercorns
1 small bay leaf
4 spring onions, roughly chopped
100 g mushrooms, sliced
2 tablespoons butter
3 tablespoons plain flour
⅔ cup (150 ml) milk
2 egg yolks
⅔ cup (150 ml) cream
salt and pepper
fresh lemon juice
2 potatoes, cooked and mashed
5 tablespoons grated Swiss cheese
5 tablespoons fresh breadcrumbs
extra 1 tablespoon butter

1 Wipe scallops, separate roe and slice scallop meat.

2 Combine wine, peppercorns, bay leaf, spring onions and mushrooms in a pan and bring to the boil. Reduce heat and simmer for 2 to 3 minutes. Add scallops and enough water to cover. Cook over a gentle heat for 3 to 5 minutes or until tender. Remove scallops and keep warm. Simmer cooking liquid until reduced to 1¼ cups (300 ml). Strain.

3 Melt butter, add flour and cook for 2 minutes. Gradually add cooking liquid and milk. Bring to the boil, stirring, then simmer for 5 minutes.

4 Combine egg yolks and cream and add ½ cup (125 ml) of the hot sauce to the cream. Gradually pour back into sauce and heat through; do not boil. Taste and adjust seasoning with salt, pepper and lemon juice.

5 Divide scallops between four scallop shells or individual serving dishes and cover with some sauce. Pipe mashed potato around the edge of the dish and brush with a little milk.

6 Mix the cheese and breadcrumbs and sprinkle over the sauce. Dot with butter and cook under a preheated grill until lightly browned and hot. Serve remaining sauce separately.

SERVES 4

SCALLOPS *in* SAFFRON CREAM SAUCE

500 g scallops
pinch saffron threads
1 egg yolk
90 g grated fresh Parmesan cheese
1½ tablespoons cream
salt and white pepper
60 g butter
3 tablespoons whisky or sherry
fresh dill and cherry tomatoes, to garnish

1 Preheat oven to 200°C (400°F).

2 Clean scallops, separating roe and meat.

3 Place saffron in a small heatproof bowl and pour over 1 tablespoon boiling water, allow to cool, then squeeze threads well.

4 Crush roe of scallops to a paste using a mortar and pestle, fork or blender. Add saffron, egg yolk, cheese, cream and season to taste with salt and pepper. Stir well to combine.

5 Melt butter, add scallops and cook over a high heat for 1 minute stirring constantly. Add whisky and heat through.

6 Divide contents of pan between four individual serving dishes or scallop shells. Pour cream mixture over and bake for 20 minutes. Serve garnished with sprays of dill and cherry tomatoes.

SERVES 4

STUFFED MUSSELS

1 kg mussels

500 g English spinach or silverbeet

4 anchovy fillets

milk

1 egg, hard-boiled

1 clove garlic, crushed

juice 1 lemon

90 to 125 g butter

pinch grated nutmeg

ground black pepper

1 cup (60 g) fresh white breadcrumbs

60 g grated fresh Parmesan cheese

watercress leaves (optional)

lemon wedges

1 Preheat oven to 200°C (400°F).

2 Scrub mussels with a hard brush and using a small sharp knife pull out and discard the beard. Discard mussels that will not stay shut.

3 Wash spinach well, discard stalks and shred leaves. Pack into a pan, cover and cook over a low heat until tender. Drain well and when cooled, squeeze out as much liquid as possible. Chop very finely.

4 Soak anchovy fillets in milk for 10 minutes. Drain well. Add egg and anchovies to spinach with garlic and blend well.

5 Mix lemon juice, 90 g butter, nutmeg and pepper. Pour onto spinach and beat well until smooth. Add more butter if necessary. Add sufficient breadcrumbs to form a stiff mixture. Taste and adjust seasoning.

6 Wrap one hand in a tea towel and with the other, open mussels by inserting a short strong sharp knife near the hinge, twisting the knife quickly to open the shell. Break off and discard the top shell.

7 Spread about 1 tablespoon of spinach mixture over each mussel and smooth with a knife dipped in water. Sprinkle with the Parmesan cheese and bake for 10 to 12 minutes or until browned.

SERVES 4

Pull out and discard beard.

Add egg and anchovies to spinach in blender.

Wrap one hand in tea towel and open mussels with knife.

SERVING STUFFED MUSSELS

Serve these stuffed mussels on a bed of watercress leaves and garnished with lemon wedges.

Chilled Mussel Salad

CHILLED MUSSEL SALAD

2 kg mussels, in shells

1 cup (250 ml) wine

1 cup (250 ml) water

few sprigs parsley

3 bay leaves

1 teaspoon black peppercorns

DRESSING

3 tablespoons white wine vinegar

salt and pepper

1 teaspoon French mustard

¾ cup (180 ml) oil

4 eggs, hard-boiled

3 tablespoons chopped fresh parsley

1 teaspoon chopped fresh tarragon

1 teaspoon snipped chives

2 teaspoons chopped gherkins

1 Scrub mussels well and discard any with open shells. With a vegetable knife, remove the beard.

2 Bring the wine, water, parsley, bay leaves and peppercorns to the boil in a large saucepan then lower heat and simmer for 5 minutes.

3 Add the mussels, cover and simmer until they open, about 3 to 5 minutes. Now remove the mussels from their shells, pouring off any cooking liquid or pieces of flavouring. Arrange the mussels in individual serving dishes, discarding any that do not open.

4 TO PREPARE DRESSING: Whisk vinegar, salt, pepper and mustard well to combine. Gradually add the oil, whisking constantly. Taste and adjust the seasoning.

5 Chop the hard-boiled eggs and add to the dressing with the parsley, tarragon, chives and gherkins, stirring to combine. Leave for 30 minutes for the flavours to be absorbed. Stir again then pour evenly over the mussels.

6 Toss lightly so that all the mussels are coated with the dressing then chill until serving time. Serve with crusty bread and lemon wedges.

SERVES 4 TO 6

STEAMED MUSSELS

1 kg New Zealand mussels

30 g butter

1 clove garlic, crushed

1 small onion, chopped

6 peppercorns

1 sprig parsley

1 small bay leaf

1¼ cups (300 ml) dry white wine

3 tablespoons red wine vinegar

500 g white fish, cubed

⅔ cup (150 ml) cream

2 egg yolks

½ teaspoon cornflour

4 tablespoons chopped fresh parsley

salt and pepper

juice ½ lemon

1 Scrub mussels and remove the beard. Discard mussels that do not stay shut.

2 Melt butter in large covered dish and cook garlic and onion until onion is soft. Add mussels, peppercorns, parsley, bay leaf, wine and vinegar. Cover and bring to the boil. Simmer until mussels open. Remove mussels and add fish to stock. Simmer until cooked.

3 Remove mussels from shells and discard shells. Place mussels on a serving plate and keep warm. Strain cooking liquid into small saucepan and reserve. Blend cream, egg yolks and cornflour until smooth.

4 Heat cooking liquid until boiling. Add ½ cup (125 ml) of the hot liquid to the cream mixture and stir well. Pour back into pan and heat gently until sauce thickens slightly. Do not boil.

5 Stir half the parsley through sauce. Taste and adjust seasoning with salt and pepper and sharpen to taste with lemon juice. Pour sauce over mussels and sprinkle with remaining parsley. Serve hot with steamed new potatoes and broccoli.

SERVES 4

BARBECUED MUSSELS

Place mussels directly onto a heated barbecue plate (after removing beard from mussels). Blend some butter, parsley and garlic and as mussels start to open, spoon the butter onto and into them. Remove mussels when they are fully open. Serve with rice or noodles.

Steamed Mussels

HERBED TOMATO SAUCE

Heat 3 tablespoons olive oil and sauté a finely chopped onion for 5 minutes. Add 2 crushed cloves garlic and a finely chopped red capsicum (pepper) and sauté a further 2 minutes. Add 1 kg tomatoes (finely chopped), 3 bay leaves, 2½ teaspoons sugar, 2 teaspoons finely chopped basil leaves, 2 teaspoons finely chopped oregano and ½ cup (125 ml) dry white wine. Simmer, stirring occasionally, for 1 hour, or until sauce thickens. Sauce may be kept in the refrigerator for 5 days, or frozen.

CURRIED MUSSELS

750 g mussels

⅔ cup (150 ml) dry white wine

1 tablespoon white vinegar

1 bouquet garni

1 clove garlic, bruised

30 g butter

1 onion, chopped

1 teaspoon curry powder

good pinch turmeric

good pinch cayenne pepper

1 tablespoon plain flour

juice 1 lemon

½ cup (125 ml) thickened cream

1 Scrub mussels with a hard brush and using a small sharp knife, pull out and discard the beards. Discard mussels that will not stay closed.

2 Bring wine, vinegar, bouquet garni and garlic to the boil. Add mussels and simmer, covered, until they open, about 5 minutes. Discard mussels that do not open.

3 Remove mussels, pull off and discard top shells and keep warm. Strain cooking liquid and reserve. Heat butter and sauté onion until soft. Add curry powder, turmeric, cayenne and flour and cook, stirring, for 1 minute.

4 Gradually add reserved stock off the heat. Bring to the boil, reduce heat and simmer for 5 minutes. Stir in lemon juice and gently heat through. Add cream carefully, pour sauce over mussels and serve hot.

SERVES 4

BAKED OYSTERS

36 oysters in shell

3 tablespoons chopped fresh parsley

freshly ground black pepper

½ cup (125 ml) olive oil

3 tablespoons breadcrumbs

1½ lemons, to serve

1 Preheat oven to 160°C (325°F).

2 Arrange oysters in a single layer in an oven dish. Sprinkle parsley on top. Grind a generous quantity of pepper over them and pour on a little olive oil.

3 Add breadcrumbs, more freshly ground black pepper and the remainder of the olive oil. Bake oysters in oven for 15 minutes. Serve hot with lemon wedges.

SERVES 6

BRAISED CALAMARI *with* TOMATO SAUCE

12 small calamari (squid)

2 cloves garlic, thinly sliced

4 rolled anchovies, thinly sliced

2 hard-boiled eggs, thinly sliced

2 tablespoons Parmesan cheese

1 cup (60 g) soft white breadcrumbs

1 tablespoon chopped Italian parsley

salt and pepper

1½ cups (375 ml) Herbed Tomato Sauce (see recipe)

rolled anchovies and Italian parsley, to garnish

1 Remove heads and tentacles from hood. Remove skin from hood and flaps by pulling firmly. Flaps can be removed if desired. Using a sharp knife score the flesh into a diamond pattern, taking care not to cut all the way through. Slice tentacles thinly.

2 Add garlic, anchovies and eggs. Add cheese, breadcrumbs, parsley and seasonings. Place filling into prepared hoods and secure with toothpicks.

3 Put Herbed Tomato Sauce into pan and add calamari hoods. Cover with lid and simmer 20 to 30 minutes, turning after 15 minutes. When serving, pour enough sauce onto serving plates to lightly cover surface. Place two cooked hoods in centre and garnish each with a rolled anchovy and finely chopped parsley.

SERVES 6

Braised Calamari with Tomato Sauce

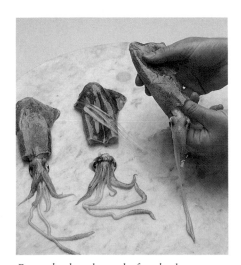

Remove heads and tentacles from hood.

Remove skin from hood and flaps by pulling firmly.

Score flesh in a diamond pattern using a sharp knife.

For this recipe, try to find true English spinach, not silverbeet.

OYSTERS ROCKEFELLER

24 oysters in the shell or bottled
rock salt
½ bunch spinach
30 to 60 g butter
6 spring onions, finely chopped
5 tablespoons chopped fresh parsley
½ cup (60 g) fine dry breadcrumbs
salt and freshly ground pepper
cayenne pepper to taste

1 Preheat oven to 230°C (450°F).

2 Separate oysters from the shell, wash and dry shells well and then place oysters back in shell. Arrange oysters in a baking dish lined with rock salt. If using bottled oysters, drain

and divide between four ovenproof dishes.

3 Separate spinach leaves and stalks, roll up leaves and shred finely. Wash and drain leaves then pack into a pan and steam, covered, until tender. Drain and finely chop.

4 Melt 30 g butter, add spring onions and cook until softened. Add spinach and remaining ingredients and stir to combine. If necessary, add remaining butter to bind mixture. Taste and adjust seasoning. Divide between oysters, bake for 7 to 10 minutes. Arrange on plates and serve immediately.

SERVES 4

Separate oysters from shells.

Divide mixture between oysters and bake in dish lined with rock salt.

MUSSELS *with* FENNEL

1 kg fresh mussels
few sprigs fresh fennel
1¼ cups (310 ml) dry white wine
½ cup (125 ml) water
bouquet garni
salt and freshly ground black pepper
6 spring onions, chopped
30 g butter
2 tablespoons plain flour

1 Scrub and rinse mussels and remove the beard using a sharp knife. Discard any mussels that are not firmly closed.

2 Place fennel, wine, water, bouquet garni, salt, pepper and spring onions in a large saucepan. Bring to the boil and add prepared mussels. Cook covered for 3 to 4 minutes or until all mussels have opened. Strain, and reserve cooking liquid, discarding bouquet garni. Place mussels in serving bowls and keep warm while making sauce.

3 Melt butter in rinsed out pan and add flour. Cook over moderate heat, stirring for a minute. Pour over the reserved cooking liquid, whisking constantly. Cook until sauce has slightly thickened. Spoon over mussels. Serve at once garnished with fennel.

SERVES 4

STUFFED BAKED CALAMARI

*Take time to prepare this delicious dish.
Try it at least once, and your family will ask you
for a repeat performance!*

800 g calamari (squid), 15 cm hood is ideal
1 clove garlic, finely chopped
1 small bunch parsley, finely chopped
2 to 3 tablespoons fresh breadcrumbs
olive oil
salt and pepper
1 egg yolk
3 tablespoons dry white wine

1 Preheat oven to 180°C (350°F).
2 Clean the calamari, but leave head intact. Chop the tentacles finely and place in a bowl with garlic and parsley.
3 Add the breadcrumbs, a tablespoon of olive oil, salt and pepper, and egg yolk. Stuff the heads with this mixture and close them with a toothpick.
4 Arrange the stuffed calamari in an oven dish, moisten with melted butter or oil and sprinkle a little white wine and some salt and pepper on top. Bake for 40 to 50 minutes. Serve hot.

SERVES 4

BARBECUED OCTOPUS

500 g small octopus

MARINADE
½ cup (125 ml) olive oil
3 tablespoons fresh lemon juice
1 clove garlic, crushed
2 tablespoons chopped fresh parsley

1 Clean octopus by cutting vertically through one side of the head and tentacles. Remove sacs from the head and the 'beak' (this is a hard shell piece located at the centre where the tentacles join), discard these parts. Wash octopus under clean water.
2 Combine olive oil, lemon juice, garlic and parsley, mixing well.
3 Place octopus onto barbecue plate and brush generously with marinade. Cook for approximately 10 minutes.
4 Serve with a fresh herb and lettuce salad.
NOTE: The octopus will curl and then turn a claret red colour, which looks most attractive in a garden salad. Occasionally even the small octopus can be tough. You can tenderise before cooking by steaming for approximately 4 to 5 minutes.

SERVES 4

Stuffed Baked Calamari

Finely chop tentacles, garlic and parsley.

Combine ingredients for stuffing.

Stuff heads and close with a toothpick.

Freshwater FISH

Most of the recipes in this section specify trout or salmon, but you can substitute Murray perch, silver perch, golden perch or Murray cod. Whitefish can be substituted for trout, and salmon trout is prepared like salmon. However, both trout and salmon are now readily available — trout is available all year in the southern hemisphere and in March to September in the northern hemisphere. Salmon is in season in winter in the southern hemisphere and March to October in the northern hemisphere.

Both salmon and trout can be bought whole or filleted, smoked or unsmoked. Cutlets are usually ideal for serving sizes. Freshwater fish are delicious when poached or baked, and served with creamy sauces, herbs and spices and because of their mild flavour, take on the flavours which are added. They can be served hot or cold. They can be cooked in many other ways and the best thing about them is that they are very hard to ruin by overcooking!

SALMON CUTLETS
with SORREL SAUCE

4 to 6 salmon cutlets (150 to 200 g each)

freshly ground black pepper

60 g unsalted butter

SORREL CREAM SAUCE

60 g unsalted butter

2 spring onions, chopped

1 cup (250 ml) crème fraîche

juice ½ lemon

8 sorrel leaves

salt and freshly ground black pepper

Salmon Cutlets with Sorrel Sauce, served with steamed vegetables

1 Season salmon cutlets with pepper. Heat butter in a heavy-based frying pan. Quickly cook salmon until golden, about 3 to 4 minutes on each side. This will vary depending on the thickness of the cutlets. Test by gently prying the flesh apart. If it pulls away easily, the cutlet is cooked. Be careful not to overcook the salmon.

2 TO PREPARE SAUCE: Melt butter and cook spring onions gently until softened. Add crème fraîche and lemon juice. Bring to the boil and simmer gently for 1 minute. Remove stems from sorrel and slice leaves into strips. Add to pan and cook for 2 minutes; season to taste.

3 Place salmon cutlets on a heated serving dish and spoon over the warm sauce. Serve immediately.

SERVES 4

TROUT PÂTÉ

250 g fresh salmon or trout fillets

**½ cup (125 ml) Fish Stock
(see recipe page 88)**

½ cup (125 ml) dry white wine

125 g smoked salmon

280 g unsalted butter

3 tablespoons cream

salt

freshly ground white pepper

freshly ground nutmeg

sprigs fresh dill and lemon twists, to garnish

1 Bring fillets slowly to the boil with fish stock and wine, skim, then simmer gently until just tender.

2 Allow fillets to cool in the liquid. Pick out skin and bones, cut fish into small pieces and set aside. Boil poaching liquid until it is reduced by half, then cool and add 1 tablespoon of the liquid to the fillets.

3 Cut smoked salmon into small pieces and sauté for 1 to 2 minutes in 30 g butter. Stir in cream, salt, pepper and nutmeg. Cool, and blend adding the remaining butter cut into knobs. When consistency is paste-like, combine with the very small pieces of poached fish.

4 Serve at room temperature in small pâté pots or dishes. Garnish each with a sprig of fresh dill and a lemon twist.

SERVES 6

CRÈME FRAÎCHE

Stir ¾ cup (180 ml) cream and 1 tablespoon plain yoghurt together in a jar and keep covered overnight or for 8 hours in a warm place. Alternatively, place loosely covered jar in microwave oven and cook on lowest temperature (50°C, 95°F) for 4 minutes. Before using chill well. It will thicken as it chills.

TROUT *with* RED WINE SAUCE

4 trout, gutted

salt and pepper

4 tablespoons water

4 peppercorns

SAUCE

50 g butter

1 small onion, finely chopped

½ carrot, finely chopped

1 cup (250 ml) red wine

1 sprig fresh thyme

3 teaspoons plain flour

¼ to ½ teaspoon anchovy essence

1 tablespoon chopped fresh parsley

1 Preheat oven to 180°C (350°F).

2 Wipe trout and season lightly with pepper. Grease baking dish, lay in trout and add water and peppercorns.

3 Cover trout with a piece of buttered greaseproof paper and bake in preheated oven for about 20 minutes or until fish flakes easily when tested. Remove and keep warm on a serving plate. Strain and reserve cooking liquid.

4 **TO PREPARE SAUCE:** Heat 3 teaspoons butter and sauté onion and carrot. Pour in wine and simmer until reduced by half. Stir in reserved cooking liquid and thyme and simmer for a further 5 minutes.

5 Combine 1 tablespoon butter with the flour and add to pan in pieces. Simmer until sauce thickens. Stir in anchovy essence, remaining 3 teaspoons butter and parsley. Taste and adjust seasoning. Spoon sauce over fish and serve hot with steamed new potatoes and sautéed snow peas.

SERVES 4

TROUT COOKED IN BUTTER

This is a simple, classic way of preparing trout. The trout is rolled in seasoned flour, then cooked in clarified butter. The butter is then heated till it becomes brown, then lemon juice and parsley are added and this is poured over the fish.

STEP-BY-STEP TECHNIQUES

Trout with Almonds

TROUT *with* ALMONDS

4 trout, gutted

⅓ cup (40 g) plain flour

salt and pepper

110 g butter

4 tablespoons oil

60 g flaked almonds

lemon slices, to garnish

1 Wipe fish with a damp cloth. Season flour with salt and pepper. Dip fish in seasoned flour and pat off excess.

2 Heat 90 g butter and the oil in a frying pan and fry trout on both sides until cooked, about 7 to 10 minutes depending on thickness. Remove to a serving plate and keep warm.

3 Clean frying pan and heat 20 g butter. Add almonds and cook until golden. Sprinkle over trout and garnish with lemon slices. Serve hot with French beans.

SERVES 4

Dip fish in seasoned flour, pat off excess.

Fry trout on both sides until cooked.

MARINATED TROUT

2 tablespoons coarse salt

2 tablespoons sugar

1 tablespoon white peppercorns, crushed

1 bunch fresh dill, coarsely chopped

500 g trout, cut into 2 fillets

DANISH MUSTARD SAUCE

brown sugar

prepared French mustard

1 Combine salt, sugar and peppercorns. Take a sheet of foil, large enough to securely wrap and cover fish, and place on a work surface.

2 Sprinkle a little of the salt mixture over foil then cover with a little dill. Place one trout fillet, skin side down, over the dill. Cover trout with most of the remaining dill and salt mixture and top with remaining fillet, dill and salt mixture.

3 Press down firmly with your hands. Wrap trout up in foil and secure well. Place in a lamington tin and weigh down using 3 or 4 cans of food.

4 Refrigerate for 2 days, turning trout several times. Remove from foil, scrape off seasonings and cut into serving pieces. Serve with brown bread and butter and Danish mustard sauce.

5 TO PREPARE SAUCE: Combine equal amounts of brown sugar and prepared mustard, stir well and serve sprinkled with chopped dill.

SERVES 4 (AS AN ENTRÉE)

GRILLED TROUT

Suitable for a large fish, grilling is also a good way to prepare the more oily-fleshed varieties such as mullet. If you do not wish to use a barbecue or griller, fish prepared in this way is also delicious baked in the oven.

4 trout, gutted, scaled and cleaned

fresh lemon juice

salt

pepper

olive oil

1 cup chopped fresh parsley

2 cloves garlic, crushed

2 lemons, sliced

1 Wash fish briefly and dry it carefully with absorbent paper.

2 Place fish on a plate and sprinkle with lemon juice, salt, pepper and olive oil, both outside and inside. Leave to marinate for about 15 minutes or so, turning from time to time.

3 Put the fish under a preheated grill. Start the cooking on very high heat so that the skin becomes crisp, and then lower the heat and proceed slowly until the eye turns opaque. If the fish starts to look too dry, brush with some of the marinade. Turn the fish and proceed to cook the other side in the same way. Fish is cooked when the flesh is white throughout and detaches easily from the bones.

4 Mix parsley, garlic, more salt, pepper and lots of oil.

5 When fish is cooked, arrange on a plate, sprinkle with parsley mixture, and decorate with lemon slices.

SERVES 4

 MARINATED TROUT

This is a delicious dish, tasting rather like smoked salmon. In Scandinavia, it is traditionally made with fresh salmon. Trout or salmon trout can be used instead for this version.

PRESERVES

Preserved seafood involves drying, salting or smoking, methods of preservation which have been used for a very long time. Nutrients in preserved fish are very similar to those in fresh fish but sometimes some vitamins may be lost. Canned products retain all nutrients.

Preserved seafood can usually be used as it is, but dried fish requires soaking for a day, to soften and remove some of the salt. Smoked fish will usually keep for a few days in the refrigerator, but it can be frozen for longer. Pickled and canned fish should be refrigerated after opening.

Preserved seafood is ideal for use in pâtés, mousses, soufflés and more. Their delicate flavour makes very distinctive dishes. Anchovies lift a dish without intruding on its flavour and they can be added to sauces, pasta dishes, pizza and casseroles. Crabmeat is very versatile and can be used in salads, sauces, stuffings, dips and lots more. The much relished smoked salmon can be eaten as is. Use canned salmon in pastries and quiches.

Using preserved seafood is a terrific way to satisfy your taste for seafood without the preparation required for fresh seafood.

CRABMEAT *and* SPINACH SOUP

250 g crabmeat, fresh or canned

45 g butter

1 onion, finely chopped

1 to 2 cloves garlic, crushed

1 bunch Chinese spinach or English spinach
or silver beet, roughly chopped

4 cups (1 litre) chicken stock

½ cup (125 ml) coconut milk

salt and pepper

Tabasco sauce to taste

thickened cream (optional)

1 Pick over the crabmeat, discarding any cartilage.

2 Heat butter in saucepan and sauté onion and garlic until soft. Add spinach and stir to coat with butter. Cook over a gentle heat until leaves start to wilt.

Crabmeat and Spinach Soup

3 Stir in stock and coconut milk and season with salt and pepper. Bring to the boil, reduce heat and simmer for 10 minutes or until spinach is tender.

4 Add crabmeat and heat through. Add Tabasco sauce to taste and thickened cream, if desired. Serve soup hot.

SERVES 6

DRIED COD SOUP

400 g dried salt fish

4 cups (1 litre) water

⅓ cup (80 ml) olive oil

2 cloves garlic, roughly chopped

3 onions, sliced

300 g potatoes, diced

1 bay leaf

freshly ground pepper

pinch cayenne pepper

1 Cover fish with cold water and leave to soak overnight. Drain and discard water.

2 Place fish in a saucepan and cover with water. Bring to the boil, reduce heat and simmer for 7 minutes or until fish flakes when tested. Drain and reserve cooking liquid. Flake fish and discard bones and skin.

3 Heat oil in a saucepan and sauté garlic for 3 minutes. Remove garlic and set aside. Add onions and sauté until softened. Cover with potatoes then add fish, bay leaf, pepper and cooking liquid. Bring to the boil, reduce heat and simmer, covered, for 20 minutes or until potatoes are tender.

4 Add cayenne pepper to garlic, and stir into soup. Taste and adjust seasoning; salt should not be necessary. Remove bay leaf before serving.

NOTE: This is a very salty dish. Fish can be soaked in milk instead of water to reduce saltiness.

SERVES 4 TO 6

Dried Cod Soup

CRAB SOUFFLÉ

1 tablespoon grated Parmesan cheese

200 g canned crabmeat

3 tablespoons butter

2 tablespoons plain flour

⅔ cup (150 ml) milk

½ teaspoon paprika

½ to 1 teaspoon curry powder

few drops chilli sauce

2 tablespoons cream

salt and pepper

3 egg yolks

4 egg whites

1 Preheat oven to 190°C (375°F).

2 Lightly grease a 15 cm soufflé dish and dust with Parmesan cheese.

3 Pick over the crabmeat, discarding any cartilage.

4 Heat 2 tablespoons butter in a pan. Sprinkle over flour and cook for 1 minute, stirring continuously. Off the heat, gradually add milk. Bring to the boil, reduce heat and simmer, stirring for 2 minutes. Set white sauce aside.

5 Heat remaining butter in a frying pan and fry paprika and curry powder for 1 minute. Add crabmeat and chilli sauce and stir to mix well.

6 Stir crab mixture through white sauce, and add cream, and salt and pepper to taste. Stir through egg yolks one at a time.

7 Whisk egg whites until stiff. Gently fold whites into crab mixture. Pour into prepared dish and bake for 20 to 25 minutes or until well risen and firm. Serve with a green salad.

SERVES 4

 CRABMEAT

Canned crab is available all over the world. After opening, it should be stored in the refrigerator and used within 24 hours.

STEP-BY-STEP TECHNIQUES

Combine breadcrumbs, cheese and parsley.

Add crabmeat and remaining ingredients.

Divide between individual serving dishes.

DEVILLED CRAB

250 g crabmeat, canned or fresh

2 tablespoons butter

6 spring onions, finely chopped

2 tablespoons dry sherry

60 g fresh white breadcrumbs

few drops Tabasco sauce

½ teaspoon Worcestershire sauce

1 teaspoon French mustard

salt and pepper

knobs of butter

lemon slices and watercress sprigs, to garnish

TOPPING

2 tablespoons fresh white breadcrumbs

2 tablespoons grated fresh Parmesan cheese

2 tablespoons chopped fresh parsley

1 Preheat oven to 200°C (400°F).

2 Pick over crabmeat, discarding any cartilage.

3 TO PREPARE TOPPING: Combine breadcrumbs, cheese and parsley. Set aside.

4 Heat butter in a small pan. Add spring onions and cook until soft. Add crabmeat, sherry, breadcrumbs, Tabasco and Worcestershire sauces, mustard and salt and pepper to taste. Stir well to combine. Heat through over a low heat.

5 Divide between four individual serving dishes or scallop shells. Sprinkle with topping. Put several knobs of butter on each dish and bake for 10 minutes. Serve garnished with lemon slices and watercress sprigs.

SERVES 4

ANCHOVY *and* EGG MOUSSE

8 canned anchovy fillets

milk

**⅓ cup (80 ml) Mayonnaise
(see recipe page 89)**

2 tablespoons cream

2 tablespoons chopped fresh parsley

1 teaspoon anchovy essence (optional)

chilli sauce

ground white pepper

4 eggs, hard-boiled

1 egg white

watercress leaves, to garnish

1 Cover anchovies in milk and allow to soak for 10 minutes. Drain well.

2 In a blender or food processor, combine anchovies with mayonnaise, cream, parsley, anchovy essence, chilli sauce and pepper to taste. Add boiled eggs and beat well to combine. Taste and adjust the seasonings.

3 Whisk egg white until stiff. Fold into anchovy mixture using a spatula. Spoon into a serving dish and level the top. Cover with plastic wrap and refrigerate for several hours.

4 Garnish with watercress and serve with sticks of celery, carrot, spring onions, wedges of cucumber and button mushrooms.

SERVES 4

SALMON *and* CHIVE CREAM CHEESE

420 g canned red salmon

200 g cream cheese, at room temperature

2 tablespoons sour cream

1 tablespoon fresh lemon juice

1 bunch spring onions, chopped

2 bunches chives, snipped

freshly ground black pepper

⅓ cup (40 g) walnut or pecan pieces

1 Drain salmon and remove any skin and bones. Flake into large pieces.

2 Beat cream cheese, sour cream and lemon juice together until smooth, but still firm. Add spring onions, a quarter of the chives and season with pepper. Fold through nuts and salmon. If the mixture is very soft, chill until firm enough to handle.

3 Place salmon mixture onto a sheet of plastic wrap or greaseproof paper. Roll up into a log. Chill until quite firm. Place the remaining snipped chives on a clean sheet of greaseproof paper. Unwrap the salmon log and roll in the chives to evenly coat. Serve with crackers and crisp vegetables.

Alternatively, spoon the mixture into a serving bowl and cover the surface with snipped chives.

SERVES 4 TO 6

WATERCRESS *and* SMOKED SALMON LOGS

1 long French breadstick, split lengthways

**¾ cup (180 ml) Mayonnaise
(see recipe page 89)**

300 g smoked salmon slices

1 Spanish onion, thinly sliced

freshly ground black pepper

2 cups watercress sprigs

2 to 3 tablespoons vinaigrette

3 tablespoons fresh dill sprigs

1 Remove some of the bread centre. Spread halves thickly with mayonnaise. Lay smoked salmon over each half, top with onion and season with pepper.

2 Toss watercress sprigs in vinaigrette. Cover both halves then sprinkle with dill.

3 Press halves together and wrap securely with foil. Chill until required. To serve, separate the halves and cut into 10 cm lengths.

SERVES 4

HERB VINAIGRETTE

Place 1 tablespoon Dijon mustard in a bowl. Whisk in 1½ tablespoons white wine vinegar and 1½ tablespoons fresh chopped herbs (parsley, chives, thyme). Gradually whisk in ⅓ cup (80 ml) olive oil until mixture thickens. Season to taste.

MAYONNAISE

In recipes requiring the addition of mayonnaise, it is best to make your own, however if time is short, commercial mayonnaise is fine. You could liven it up with the addition of lemon juice, mustard, Tabasco sauce or anything else you like.

Salmon in Pastry

SALMON *in* PASTRY

**SALMON
IN PASTRY**

*To make this dish extra
special, brioche dough
can be used instead of
puff pastry.*

60 g butter

1 onion, finely chopped

2 cups cooked long grain rice

60 g Chinese vermicelli (optional)

2 x 375 g pkts frozen puff pastry, thawed

1 egg yolk, beaten

250 g canned salmon, drained and flaked

100 g mushrooms, sliced

2 hard-boiled eggs, quartered

2 tablespoons chopped fresh parsley

juice 1 lemon

1 Preheat oven to 200°C (400°F).

2 Heat butter in a pan and sauté onion until
soft. Off the heat, add rice, mix thoroughly.

3 Cover vermicelli with hot water and leave
until softened. Bring a pan of water to the
boil, add vermicelli and cook until tender.
Drain well then cut into pieces.

4 Roll out one packet of pastry to a
rectangle shape, 6 mm thick. Trim corners
to create a fish shape and place on a baking
sheet covered with buttered foil. Brush edges
of pastry with some of the egg yolk. Arrange
half the rice over pastry, leaving a 1.5 cm
border all the way round. Top rice with
salmon, vermicelli, mushrooms, boiled eggs
and parsley. Sprinkle with lemon juice then
spread remaining rice on top. Brush border
with beaten egg.

5 Roll out remaining pastry and cut to the
same shape but 3 cm larger. Carefully lift up
and arrange to cover pastry and filling.
Press down to seal edges and trim pastry a
little if necessary. Brush pastry with
remaining egg and score with a knife to
make a fish scale pattern.

6 Bake for 30 minutes or until golden.
Serve hot with sour cream and red salad.

SERVES 6 TO 8

Smoked Fish Flan

250 g smoked fish

1 small onion, sliced

4 tablespoons water

4 tablespoons dry sherry

250 g shortcrust pastry

30 g butter

2 tablespoons plain flour

1 cup (250 ml) milk

salt and pepper

pinch paprika

fresh lemon juice

1 egg, beaten

½ teaspoon anchovy essence

1 tablespoon chopped fresh parsley

1 Preheat oven to 200°C (400°F).

2 Place fish, onion, water and sherry in a saucepan. Bring to the boil, reduce heat and simmer for 10 minutes or until fish flakes when tested.

3 Remove fish and flake, discarding any bones. Roll out pastry and use to line a 23 cm flan ring. Bake blind for 15 minutes. Remove flan case and reduce oven temperature to 180°C (350°F).

4 Melt butter, add flour and cook, stirring continuously, for 2 minutes. Off the heat, gradually add milk and bring to the boil, stirring. Reduce heat and simmer for 5 minutes.

5 Season sauce with salt, pepper, paprika and lemon juice to taste.

6 Brush base of pastry with a little egg. Stir remaining egg, essence and parsley into sauce. Spread fish over base and pour over sauce. Bake for 20 minutes. Serve hot or cold with a tossed green salad.

SERVES 4 TO 6

Smoked Salmon Quiche

125 g smoked salmon, thinly sliced

PASTRY

2 cups (250 g) plain flour

½ teaspoon salt

125 g butter

1 egg yolk

1 tablespoon iced water

CUSTARD

1¼ cups (300 ml) cream

4 egg yolks

salt

cayenne pepper

grated nutmeg

1 TO MAKE PASTRY: Sift flour and salt into a basin. Cut butter into small cubes and rub into flour until the mixture resembles fine breadcrumbs. Make a well in the centre, add the egg yolk and water to form a dough. Handle as little and as lightly as possible to keep it cool and manageable. Cover with plastic wrap and chill 30 minutes.

2 Preheat oven to 180°C (350°F).

3 Roll out pastry and line one large or several small lightly greased pie plates or quiche dishes.

4 Blend custard ingredients together and pour into pastry shell. Lightly float the salmon slices over the surface. With a teaspoon, carefully spoon some of the custard over the salmon but do not let the slices sink. Bake for 40 to 45 minutes. Let the quiche stand about 4 minutes before serving.

SERVES 6 TO 8

SMOKED SALMON

This is available in sides or sliced and is usually bought vacuum packed. It can be stored in the refrigerator for about 10 days after opening.

BAKE BLIND

This term is used to bake an empty pastry case. Usually some dried peas are put in it to maintain the shape of the pastry.

 **FISH ROE PÂTÉ**

Smoked cod's roe (tarama) is available either loose or canned from larger supermarkets and delicatessens. As it is salty, there is no need to add salt during the preparation. If mixture still seems too salty when oil has been incorporated, add more bread.

Fish Roe Pâté

FISH ROE PÂTÉ

5 thick slices white bread

1 small clove garlic, crushed

150 g tarama (smoked cod's roe)

1 pickling onion, roughly chopped

juice 2 to 3 lemons

½ to 1 cup (125 to 250 ml) olive oil

black olives, to garnish

1 Remove crusts from bread then tear bread into pieces. Soak in water for a few minutes, drain and squeeze well.

2 Place bread, garlic, tarama, onion and most of the lemon juice in a blender or food processor. Process until smooth. With the machine running, gradually add half the oil.

3 Taste and adjust seasoning with lemon juice and check consistency. The mixture should be pale and creamy. Continue adding oil to achieve correct consistency. Spoon into a shallow serving dish, cover and chill.

4 Serve garnished with a few olives, with crusty bread, Melba toast or crackers.

SERVES 4 TO 6

MACKEREL PÂTÉ

4 smoked mackerel fillets or 2 whole smoked mackerel

juice 2 limes or 1 lemon

125 g packet cream cheese, softened

200 g butter, melted

pepper

sprigs of fresh herbs (dill, fennel, flat-leaved parsley)

lemon slices, to garnish

1 Skin and flake the mackerel. Place in a blender or food processor with lime or lemon juice, cream cheese and butter. Blend or process to a purée. Season to taste with pepper.

2 Turn into a suitable sized serving dish and chill for several hours. Garnish with sprigs of fresh herbs and lemon slices. Serve with Melba toast or crackers.

SERVES 4 TO 6

SMOKED TROUT PÂTÉ

3 medium smoked trout

60 g butter, softened

3 slices white bread, crusts removed

3 tablespoons milk

150 g cream cheese

½ teaspoon anchovy essence

juice ½ lemon

salt and freshly ground black pepper

1 Remove head, skin and all bones from trout and purée flesh in a food processor or blender. Gradually add butter and blend well.

2 Soak bread in milk for 5 minutes, then squeeze out excess milk and add bread and all remaining ingredients to puréed fish, blending constantly.

3 Spoon mixture into well-oiled mould, approximately 2 cup (500 ml) capacity. Refrigerate overnight. Unmould pâté and serve.

SERVES 6 TO 8

SMOKED EEL SALAD

250 g smoked eel

250 g potatoes, cooked, peeled and diced

2 heads Belgian endive (witloof)

1 tablespoon snipped chives

6 radishes, sliced

walnut halves, to garnish

DRESSING

grated rind and juice 1 large lemon

½ cup (125 ml) light sour cream

1 to 2 tablespoons grated horseradish

Tabasco sauce

salt and pepper

1 TO PREPARE DRESSING: Combine lemon juice, sour cream and horseradish. Add Tabasco sauce, and salt and pepper to taste. Chill until ready to use.

2 Remove skin from eel and slice meat off the bone in bite-sized pieces. Place eel, potatoes, endive, chives and radishes in a bowl. Pour over the dressing and toss lightly but thoroughly. Serve garnished with walnuts.

SERVES 4

Smoked Eel Salad

SMOKED EEL SALAD

If smoked eel is unavailable from your delicatessen, substitute smoked trout garnished with a little smoked salmon and sprigs of dill.

Fresh Herb Fettuccine *with* Smoked Salmon *and* Asparagus

Pasta

2½ cups (300 g) plain flour or
1¼ cups (150 g) plain flour and 1¼ cups
(200 g) semolina

pinch salt

2 teaspoons chopped fresh parsley

2 teaspoons chopped fresh basil

2 eggs

Sauce

350 g fresh asparagus spears, trimmed,
peeled and halved

30 g butter

150 g sliced smoked salmon, cut into strips

1 cup (250 ml) cream

freshly ground black pepper

1 To Prepare Pasta: Pile flour and salt on a work surface and make a well in the middle. Add parsley, basil and eggs and begin to incorporate into the flour, using a fork. When you have a loosely coherent dough, use your hands and knead it, adding a little flour or water if necessary for it to become smooth and elastic. Knead for at least 6 minutes and then rest, covered with plastic or a damp cloth, for 30 minutes.

2 Divide the dough in two and roll each half out into a thin even sheet using a rolling pin or a hand-cranked pasta machine. Rest again, covered, for 10 minutes before cutting the sheets into long thin fettuccine strips. Set aside but only cover if you feel the pasta will crack before cooking it.

3 To Prepare Sauce: In a large saucepan of boiling water put the bottom halves of the asparagus. Boil for a minute before adding the tops and continue to cook until tender. Remove with a slotted spoon and rinse under cold water. Drain, and when cool enough to handle, cut each half into halves again, discarding any woody sections. Top up the pan of water and bring back to the boil. Begin cooking the fettuccine.

4 In a large frying pan melt butter and add smoked salmon. Sauté gently for 30 seconds before adding cream. Increase the heat a little and cook to thicken, then add black pepper generously and toss in the asparagus.

5 When the pasta is 'al dente', drain and transfer to the pan with the sauce. Toss through, then serve with freshly grated Parmesan (optional) and the pepper mill handed around the table.

Serves 4 (as an entrée)

Smoked Eel *and* Fish Terrine

250 g lemon sole or flounder fillets, skinned
and boned

2 tablespoons white wine

1 tablespoon chopped fresh parsley

salt and white pepper

1 tablespoon oil

200 g button mushrooms, finely chopped

3 spring onions, finely chopped

30 g trimmed spinach

30 g watercress leaves

15 g sorrel leaves

15 g tarragon leaves

15 g flat-leaved parsley

130 g gemfish or hake fillets,
cut into small pieces

100 g smoked eel, skinned and boned

1 egg

3 teaspoons gelatine

1 Cut lemon sole or flounder fillets into strips about 6 mm thick and place in a bowl. Combine wine, parsley, salt and pepper, pour over fish and marinate for 1 hour.

2 Heat oil and fry mushrooms and spring onions until tender. Drain and purée in a blender or food processor and set aside.

3 Blanch spinach and herbs in boiling water for 2 minutes. Refresh under cold water and drain well.

4 Set oven temperature to moderately hot 190°C (375°F).

5 Place herb mixture, gemfish, eel, egg and salt and pepper to taste in a food processor. Blend until smooth.

6 In a 3 cup (750 ml) terrine or other suitable sized ovenproof dish, arrange a layer of puréed fish mixture. Top with a layer of drained fish fillets and mushroom mixture. Continue layers, finishing with puréed fish. Smooth the top.

7 Cover with a piece of greased greaseproof paper and place in a baking dish containing water. Bake for 1 hour or until terrine is firm to the touch. Remove and cool.

8 Tilt terrine and drain off cooking liquid. Measure and make up to 1 cup (250 ml) with wine, fish stock or water. Sprinkle gelatine over 3 tablespoons of the liquid and leave until water is absorbed. Dissolve over gentle heat and stir into liquid. Pour into terrine dish to fill sides and just cover top. Refrigerate until set.

9 Unmould terrine onto a serving dish and garnish with sprigs of fresh herbs. Serve cut in slices with Melba toast.

SERVES 6

SMOKED EEL

When buying eel look for a firm skin. It can be bought whole or as cutlets. Store in the refrigerator for 7 to 10 days, wrapped in foil or kept in an airtight container. Don't wrap in plastic as it will sweat.

Smoked Eel and Fish Terrine

This is a traditional rice dish from England that was served as part of the Victorian breakfast. It used to be kept warm on the sideboard with the kidneys, eggs and bacon. It is a suitable dish though for main meals, or as as accompaniment to other dishes, especially for an Indian meal.

KEDGEREE

1 cup (150 g) long grain rice

1 teaspoon curry powder

500 g smoked fish fillets

salt and pepper

2 eggs, hard-boiled and chopped

juice 1 lemon

2 tablespoons chopped parsley

60 g butter, melted

extra 30 g butter

1 Preheat oven to 180°C (350°F).

2 Wash rice well then place in a pan and cover with 2.5 cm water. Sprinkle curry powder over and stir well. Bring to the boil, reduce heat to medium and cook until water has evaporated. Cover tightly with lid, turn heat to lowest point and cook, without lifting lid, for 7 minutes. Remove from heat.

3 While the rice is cooking, cook the fish. Place in a frying pan and cover with water. Bring to the boil, reduce heat and simmer until fillets are tender and flake when tested. Drain and flake fish.

4 Combine rice and fish with remaining ingredients except the extra butter. Taste and adjust seasoning. Place in an ovenproof dish, dot with extra butter and heat through in oven. Serve with a green salad.

SERVES 4 TO 6

NEAPOLITAN PIZZA

DOUGH

4 cups (500 g) plain flour

30 g fresh yeast

salt

2 tablespoons oil

TOPPING

500 g tomatoes, fresh or canned, peeled and coarsely chopped

2 small mozzarellas or 1 large one

35 g canned anchovies

fresh or dried oregano

olive oil

1 TO PREPARE DOUGH: Sift the flour on to a bench, make a small well in the centre and crumble in the yeast. Mix with a little warm and slightly salted water and the oil, until you have a rather soft dough. Knead the dough until it is smooth and elastic and does not stick to the working surface. Form a ball and with a knife cut a cross on its top, to facilitate the rising process. Cover with a clean towel and put in a warm place until it has risen to twice its volume (probably 3 hours).

2 Preheat oven to 225°C (425°F).

3 Flour your working surface and knead the dough again for several minutes. Divide the dough into four and roll each piece out to a thickness of 1 cm or less to form four pizzas. Slightly oil a flat oven tray and place the pizzas on it.

4 Cover the pizzas with the chopped tomatoes and then arrange thick slices of mozzarella on top. Decorate with anchovies in a criss-cross pattern, sprinkle generously with oregano and olive oil and cook in oven for 30 to 40 minutes. Serve immediately.

SERVES 4

PANCAKES *with* CAVIAR

⅔ cup (150 ml) water

⅔ cup (150 ml) milk

**10 g compressed yeast
(½ teaspoon dry yeast)**

¾ cup (90 g) plain flour

¾ cup (100 g) wholemeal flour

2 eggs, beaten

a little oil

200 g caviar, lumpfish roe or salmon caviar

⅔ cup (150 ml) sour cream

1 Heat water and milk until lukewarm (slightly warmer if using dry yeast). If milk overheats, cook to lukewarm before adding yeast. Add yeast to milk and stir gently to dissolve. Leave in a warm place until frothy.

2 Sift flours twice, returning husks to bowl. Make a well in the centre and pour in yeast mixture and eggs. Using a wooden spoon, blend in flour until a smooth batter is formed. Cover and leave in a warm place for 1 hour.

3 Stir batter for 10 seconds.

4 Lightly grease a heavy-based frying pan with oil. Cook pancakes on both sides, allowing approximately 2 tablespoons batter for each one. Drain pancakes and keep warm.

5 Serve hot with caviar and chilled sour cream in separate dishes.

SERVES 4 TO 6

Pancakes with Caviar

HERRINGS *in* SOUR CREAM

2 x 150 g jars herrings

1 cup (250 ml) sour cream

2 tablespoons white wine vinegar

½ teaspoon sugar

1 onion, sliced in fine rings

1 Drain herrings and check for bones. Cut herrings into strips about 2.5 cm wide and arrange on individual serving dishes.

2 Combine sour cream, vinegar and sugar. Spoon over fillets and garnish with onion rings.

SERVES 4 TO 6

HERRINGS IN SOUR CREAM

This is an easy-to-prepare last minute dish for unexpected guests. Most of the ingredients will be found at home and the herrings are available from larger supermarkets or delicatessens. However if you do have time, chill for a few hours before serving.

SAUCES

 FISH STOCK

Fish stock will keep in the refrigerator for 3 days. If preferred, stock can be frozen. Freeze either in ice-cube trays or 1 cup (250 ml) quantities.

FISH STOCK

Beads, bones and trimmings of a firm-fleshed fish (snapper, whiting etc.)

1 onion, finely chopped

½ cup (125 ml) white wine

4 sprigs parsley, roughly chopped

5 black peppercorns

juice ½ lemon

few celery leaves

6 cups (1.5 litres) water

1 Place all ingredients in a saucepan and add water to cover. Bring to the boil, reduce heat and simmer, for 20 minutes only. Skim occasionally. Strain and use as required.

MAKES ABOUT 5 CUPS (1.25 LITRES)

ANCHOVY *and* HERB BUTTER

250 g butter

5 anchovy fillets

6 tablespoons finely chopped mixed herbs, (parsley, chives, basil, chervil or marjoram)

freshly ground black pepper

grated rind and juice ½ lemon

1 Cream butter in a bowl until softened.
2 Drain oil from anchovy fillets and mash until smooth, using the back of a fork.
3 Fold through butter with herbs, black pepper, lemon rind and juice. Spoon onto a piece of plastic wrap, freezer cling film or aluminium foil. Form into a log shape and chill or freeze until required.

MAKES 1 CUP (250 G)

COMPOUND BUTTERS

MAITRE D'HOTEL BUTTER

250 g butter

2 tablespoons finely chopped fresh parsley

white pepper

fresh lemon juice

1 Beat butter until soft, add parsley, pepper and lemon juice to taste and beat again.
2 Turn butter onto a piece of plastic wrap and role into a cylindrical shape. Wrap in a clean piece of plastic wrap then aluminium foil. Freeze and cut off slices as necessary. More variations include:

MUSTARD: Omit the parsley and substitute 1 tablespoon mustard or to taste.

GARLIC: Omit parsley and substitute 4 cloves garlic, crushed or to taste.

COURT BOUILLON

5 cups (1.25 litres) water

1 large carrot, sliced

1 onion, sliced

1 bay leaf

peppercorns

few sprigs parsley

2 tablespoons white wine vinegar or juice ½ large lemon

salt

1 Place all ingredients in a non-aluminium pan. Bring to simmering point and cook for 10 minutes, uncovered, to reduce. Cool. Strain and use for poaching fish as required.

MAKES 5 CUPS (1.25 LITRES)

 COURT BOUILLON

This is a poaching stock for cooking fish. White wine can be used instead of vinegar and extra herbs and celery added if the fish is not particularly well flavoured. The cooked fish can be served with a tomato, mustard or other piquant sauce.

NANTUA SAUCE

1 shell of cooked crayfish
100 g butter
1 carrot, diced
1 onion, finely chopped
2 rashers bacon, rinds removed and diced
3 tablespoons brandy
3 tablespoons dry white wine
4 tomatoes, peeled, seeded and chopped
3 tablespoons tomato purée
1 tablespoon plain flour
1 cup (250 ml) Fish Stock (see recipe page 88)
salt and cayenne pepper

1 Pound shell of crayfish to a powder. Beat butter until soft and gradually add sufficient powdered shell until butter becomes red. Melt butter over a very gentle heat, strain through a double thickness of muslin then set aside to chill.

2 Heat 60 g crayfish butter in a pan. Add carrot, onion and bacon and cook until onion is soft. Heat brandy, flame and pour over the vegetables, shaking pan until the flames die down. Pour in wine and simmer for 2 minutes. Add tomatoes and tomato purée.

3 Melt 1 tablespoon of the remaining crayfish butter, add flour and cook, stirring, for 2 minutes. Gradually add stock, bring to the boil, reduce heat and simmer for 5 minutes. Pour sauce into the tomato mixture and season to taste with salt and cayenne pepper.

4 Bring to the boil, reduce heat and simmer for 20 minutes, stirring occasionally.

5 Just before serving, stir through the remaining crayfish butter. Serve hot.

MAKES APPROXIMATELY 1.25 CUPS (300 ML)

MAYONNAISE

1 egg yolk
1 teaspoon mustard
1 cup (250 ml) peanut oil
salt
freshly ground white pepper
1 teaspoon white vinegar

1 Put yolk into a small deep bowl with mustard. Pour in oil little by little, stirring continuously with a wooden spoon, whisk or electric beater.

2 When mayonnaise is thick, add salt and pepper then vinegar. Cover and store in a cool place until you wish to serve it.

NOTE: If the egg yolks are very pale, a little natural egg colouring or a pinch of turmeric will enhance the final colour of the mayonnaise. A few drops of Tabasco can be added if wanted to give the mayonnaise a little more bite and an extra egg yolk can be added to make the sauce a little thicker. More variations include:

AïOLI: Add 2 cloves garlic, crushed, to egg yolks. Omit salt and continue as above.

TARTARE SAUCE: Add lemon juice and chopped capers, gherkins and parsley to taste.

TOMATO MAYONNAISE: To 1 cup (250 ml) basic mayonnaise, add 2 to 3 tablespoons tomato sauce, 1 tablespoon tomato paste and pepper to taste. Serve with cold seafood dishes.

LEMON MAYONNAISE: Prepare the mayonnaise as above but replace vinegar with juice of half a lemon or peel a fresh lemon, cut the flesh into small cubes and add to the mayonnaise at the time of serving. This is a particularly piquant, zesty sauce.

MAKES 1 CUP (250 ML)

COMPOUND BUTTERS

These are a useful standby to have in the freezer for those times when preparing a sauce is out of the question. Simply prepare the butters, freeze and cut off slices as necessary. Serve these with grilled fish. The mustard butter is delightful with grilled mullet and the garlic butter is very good with prawns.

*This very simple sauce
has a myriad uses. For
variety, add cheese or
fresh herbs or replace the
milk with stock. In
cooking, add the liquid
gradually to the roux
(the butter and flour
combination) and stir
the sauce constantly to
avoid lumps.*

BASIC WHITE SAUCE

30 g butter

1 tablespoon plain flour

1 cup (250 ml) milk

1 Melt butter in a medium-sized saucepan
and when it starts to foam, add flour,
stirring vigorously with a wooden spoon
over a low heat for 1 minute. Remove
saucepan from heat and add milk a little at a
time, stirring constantly.

2 If sauce begins turning lumpy, stop
adding milk and beat hard until the lumps
have dissolved. Continue to add milk until
all has been used.

3 Return to the heat and stir until
thickened and sauce starts to boil. Boil for
3 minutes then serve.

MAKES 1 CUP (250 ML)

WHITE WINE SAUCE

90 g butter

3 tablespoons plain flour

1 cup (250 ml) fish stock

2 tablespoons dry white wine

2 tablespoons cream

salt and cayenne pepper

few drops fresh lemon juice

1 Melt 30 g butter in a small saucepan and
add flour, stirring with a wooden spoon over
low heat for 1 to 2 minutes. When the
mixture becomes a light fawn colour, add
stock gradually and stir until boiling.

2 Simmer for 10 minutes, whisk in wine
and remove from heat.

3 Gradually beat in remaining butter and
stir in cream. Add seasonings and lemon
juice to taste. Before serving, strain sauce
through a fine sieve.

MAKES 1 CUP (250 ML)

HOLLANDAISE SAUCE

3 tablespoons white wine vinegar

5 black peppercorns

1 spring onion, chopped

½ bay leaf

3 egg yolks

**180 to 250 g unsalted butter, cut into cubes
and slightly softened**

salt and white pepper

squeeze fresh lemon juice

fresh dill, to garnish

1 Simmer vinegar, peppercorns, spring
onion and bay leaf together in a small
saucepan until the mixture reduces to
3 teaspoons. Strain and set aside.

2 Place egg yolks and 1 tablespoon butter
together in a heatproof bowl and whisk
together, adding flavoured vinegar. Place the
bowl over a saucepan of gently simmering
water, making sure that the bowl does not
touch the water.

3 Whisk sauce constantly, adding butter a
little at a time. If the butter is added too
quickly, the sauce may curdle. You may not
need all the butter but the finished sauce
should be a light, creamy colour, with a
foamy consistency and thick enough to coat
the back of a metal spoon.

4 Season to taste, add lemon juice and use
immediately over meat or seafood dishes.
Garnish with dill.

Some variations of this sauce include:

CAPERS: Add 1 tablespoon capers to each
cup (250 ml) of Hollandaise.

BEATEN EGG WHITES: Fold 2 stiffly beaten
egg whites into 1 cup (250 ml) Hollandaise.
This lightens the sauce.

MAKES 1½ TO 2 CUPS (375 TO 500 ML)

EASY BEARNAISE SAUCE

1 cup (250 ml) Basic White Sauce (see recipe page 90)

2 tablespoons wine vinegar

2 tablespoons dry white wine

1 teaspoon dried tarragon

2 teaspoons chopped white of spring onion

pinch salt

pinch white pepper

2 egg yolks, lightly beaten

2 tablespoons soft butter

1 Prepare Basic White Sauce then set it aside with a covering of greaseproof paper.

2 Simmer vinegar and wine with tarragon. spring onion and seasonings until the liquid is reduced by half, then strain.

3 Pour White Sauce over egg yolks, whisk, then add butter and the reduced liquid. Beat thoroughly and serve immediately.

MAKES 1½ CUPS (375 ML)

FRESH TOMATO SAUCE

500 g tomatoes, cored, peeled and roughly chopped

30 g butter

salt and pepper

pinch sugar

½ teaspoon chopped fresh basil

1 tablespoon tomato paste

1 Place tomatoes in a saucepan with butter, salt, pepper, sugar, basil and tomato paste, and bring to the boil.

2 Reduce the heat and simmer uncovered for 20 minutes. Strain sauce and set aside. The sauce will keep refrigerated for 10 days.

MAKES 4 CUPS (1 LITRE)

SEAFOOD SAUCE

This sauce is delicious served with oysters or other cold seafood dishes.

1¼ cups (300 ml) cream, lightly whipped

½ cup (125 ml) tomato sauce

salt and pepper

few drops fresh lemon juice

1 Gently fold all the ingredients for the sauce together and chill before serving.

MAKES 2 CUPS (500 ML)

COCKTAIL SAUCE

1 egg yolk

pinch each salt, white pepper and English mustard

2 teaspoons white vinegar

5 tablespoons olive oil

3 tablespoons tomato juice

1 Place yolk, seasonings and vinegar in a bowl and whisk until light in colour. Gradually pour in the oil, drop by drop at first, and then when most of the oil has been added, pour the oil in a little faster.

2 Taste the sauce and correct the seasonings. Stir in the tomato juice and serve with fresh seafood.

MAKES ¾ CUP (180 ML)

SPECIES	SEASONAL AVAILABILITY	FORM OF PREPARATION
Blue Swimmer Crabs	All year, mainly summer (S), Jan to Sep (N)	Whole
Bream, Sea	All year, mainly autumn	Whole
Cuttlefish	All year *	Cut into strips, or one large piece, rolled
Flathead	All year – mainly autumn	Fillets
Garfish	All year (S), all year except Jul to Aug (N)	Whole
Gemfish	Winter (S)	Fillets, cutlets (available smoked)
John Dory	All year*	Whole, fillets
Kingfish	All year, mainly autumn	Fillets, cutlets
Leatherjacket	All year	Whole (headed)
Ling	Winter	Fillets
Lobster, rock	All year, mainly summer (S), Mar to Oct (N)	Whole
Mullet	Autumn to winter (S), all year (N)	Whole fillets, roe (available smoked)
Octopus	All year *	Cut into desired pieces. Remove head
Ocean Perch	Autumn to winter (S), Jun to Dec (N)	Fillets
Pearl Perch	Autumn to winter (S), Jun to Dec (N)	Fillets
Pilchards (Sardines)	Autumn, winter, spring (S), Apr to Nov (N)	Whole
Prawns, King	All year, particularly summer	Peeled meat form. Cooked, uncooked
Prawns, Royal Red	All year	Peeled meat form
Redfish	All year, mainly spring (S)	Fillets
Scallops	All year (S), Sep to Apr (N)	Meat
Snapper	All year, mainly spring	Whole, fillets, cutlets
Spanish Mackerel	Summer (S), Dec to Jul (N)	Cutlets
Squid	All year	Cut into rings or whole 'hoods'
Tailor	Feb to May (S)	Whole fillets (available smoked)
Trevally	Summer	Fillets (should be skinned to improve flavour)
Tuna	All year, mainly autmn to winter	Cut into pieces, whole
Whiting	All year	Whole, fillets

* Species available all year in limited quantities, (S) Southern hemisphere, (N) Northern hemisphere

DESCRIPTION	IDEAL FLAVOURING AND HERBS
Sweet, white, fine textured flesh, both in body and legs. Should not feel light and hollow.	Mint, dill, parsley
White flesh, fine texture, delicate flavour. Ideally one fish per person.	Lemon thyme, sesame seeds, parsley, chives
Similar to calamari in taste. Much cheaper, though a little tougher. Marinate in lemon juice or milk for a couple of hours to tenderise.	Oregano, basil, garlic, chilli, mint, parsley, soy sauce
Flaky texture. Mild tasting. A little dry, should be kept moist.	Chives, dill, lemon pepper
Sweet tasting fish, bony. Fine white flesh.	Chives, parsley, sage
Good, firm, 'chunky' white flesh, distinct flavour. Very popular. Few bones. Ideal family fish.	Basil, oregano, lemon thyme, garlic, parsley, chilli
Fine textured with white flesh, mild flavour. Supreme table fish. No bones in fillets. Mirror Dory taste similar but are much cheaper.	Chives, dill, parsley, lemon thyme, tarragon
Excellent flavoured fish, soft white flesh. Occasionally subject to condition known as 'milky'; this is obvious when cooked. If so, fish should be returned to vendor.	Ginger, chilli, lemon pepper, soy sauce
Firm and chunky flesh. Few bones, for the fussy eater.	Parsley, chives, lemon pepper
White, moist flesh, medium texture, mild flavour, good for mincing.	Dill, basil, parsley, lemon thyme, chilli, curry
Medium-textured flesh, white, moist. Rich in flavour. Superb eating.	Parsley, chives, dill, cayenne pepper, tarragon
Oily fish, strong in flavour. Great for barbecues. Very cheap in season. Extremely popular.	Oregano, basil, marjoram, garlic
Good 'sea' flavour. Slow, moist cooking is ideal.	Garlic, parsley, basil, oregano, chilli
Slightly fatty, pleasant, mild-tasting. White flesh with lovely orange-coloured skin (leave skin on).	Chives, dill, parsley, lemon thyme, sage
Mild-tasting, fine-textured, soft, white flesh. Excellent flavour, one of the greats.	Chives, dill, parlsey
Oily dark flesh. Good, distinct flavour. Highly versatile little fish. Bones easily removed.	Fennel, oregano, basil, garlic, marjoram
Moist and rich in flavour, slightly salty taste.	Coriander, chilli, mint, garlic, curry
Very moist, ideal for all 'cooked' dishes. Sold in raw state, pink, unusual sea smell. Cheap buy.	Ginger, garlic, chilli, sesame seeds, soy sauce
Fine-textured pink flesh. Mild tasting. Some bones. Very cheap and ideal for large-scale catering.	Chives, dill, lemon thyme, nutmeg, lemon pepper, sage
Rich and moist. Very versatile. Approxmately 50 to a kilo.	Chives, parsley, garlic, basil
White flesh and medium texture. Prominent fish flavour. Large fish can be dry, also ideal for displays. Classic table fish. Insist on local for best quality.	Parsley, mint, sage
White flesh tinged with pink. Mild tasting.	Garlic, oregano, basil, parsley, chives
Delicate flavour. Can be tough if over-cooked. Best to marinate in lemon juice or milk for a couple of hours before cooking. Calamari best, but not necessary. Other varieties much cheaper.	Oregano, basil, garlic
Slightly oily, medium-textured, dark in colour. Medium-priced, popular fish. Excellent smoked.	Oregano, basil, marjoram, mustard seed
Firm, dry flesh. Subtle flavour with very few bones. Ideal family fish.	Chilli, curry, parsley
Excellent raw fish (sashimi), ideal for baking and stuffing.	Horseradish, cummin, soy sauce
Fine, white flesh. Delicate flavour.	Chives, dill, tarragon, parsley

MEASURING MADE EASY

HOW TO MEASURE LIQUIDS

METRIC	IMPERIAL	CUPS
30 ml	1 fluid ounce	1 tablespoon plus 2 teaspoons
60 ml	2 fluid ounces	¼ cup
90 ml	3 fluid ounces	
125 ml	4 fluid ounces	½ cup
150 ml	5 fluid ounces	
170 ml	5½ fluid ounces	
180 ml	6 fluid ounces	¾ cup
220 ml	7 fluid ounces	
250 ml	8 fluid ounces	1 cup
500 ml	16 fluid ounces	2 cups
600 ml	20 fluid ounces (1 pint)	2½ cups
1 litre	1¾ pints	

HOW TO MEASURE DRY INGREDIENTS

15 g	½ oz	
30 g	1 oz	
60 g	2 oz	
90 g	3 oz	
125 g	4 oz	(¼ lb)
155 g	5 oz	
185 g	6 oz	
220 g	7 oz	
250 g	8 oz	(½ lb)
280 g	9 oz	
315 g	10 oz	
345 g	11 oz	
375 g	12 oz	(¾ lb)
410 g	13 oz	
440 g	14 oz	
470 g	15 oz	
500 g	16 oz	(1 lb)
750 g	24 oz	(1½ lb)
1 kg	32 oz	(2 lb)

QUICK CONVERSIONS

5 mm	¼ inch	
1 cm	½ inch	
2 cm	¾ inch	
2.5 cm	1 inch	
5 cm	2 inches	
6 cm	2½ inches	
8 cm	3 inches	
10 cm	4 inches	
12 cm	5 inches	
15 cm	6 inches	
18 cm	7 inches	
20 cm	8 inches	
23 cm	9 inches	
25 cm	10 inches	
28 cm	11 inches	
30 cm	12 inches	(1 foot)
46 cm	18 inches	
50 cm	20 inches	
61 cm	24 inches	(2 feet)
77 cm	30 inches	

NOTE: We developed the recipes in this book in Australia where the tablespoon measure is 20 ml. In many other countries the tablespoon is 15 ml. For most recipes this difference will not be noticeable.

However, for recipes using baking powder, gelatine, bicarbonate of soda, small amounts of flour and cornflour, we suggest you add an extra teaspoon for each tablespoon specified.

USING CUPS AND SPOONS

All cup and spoon measurements are level

METRIC CUP

¼ cup	60 ml	2 fluid ounces
⅓ cup	80 ml	2½ fluid ounces
½ cup	125 ml	4 fluid ounces
1 cup	250 ml	8 fluid ounces

METRIC SPOONS

¼ teaspoon	1.25 ml
½ teaspoon	2.5 ml
1 teaspoon	5 ml
1 tablespoon	20 ml

OVEN TEMPERATURES

TEMPERATURES	CELSIUS (°C)	FAHRENHEIT (°F)	GAS MARK
Very slow	120	250	½
Slow	150	300	2
Moderately slow	160-180	325-350	3-4
Moderate	190-200	375-400	5-6
Moderately hot	220-230	425-450	7
Hot	250-260	475-500	8-9

INDEX